Misunderstandings in Cross-Cultural Communications

Interpersonal, Marketing, and Negotiations Perspectives

Bagher Fardanesh, Ph.D., MPA

Published by:
Global Ink Publishing Inc. www.globalinkpublishinginc.com

Printed in the United States of America.

DEDICATION

In memory of my father, Bozorg Fardanesh.

ABOUT THE AUTHOR

Bagher Fardanesh earned his Ph.D. in Higher Education with concentrations in marketing and management, an M.A. in Public Administration, with a concentration in economic development, and a B.S. in Business Administration, all from the University of Colorado at Boulder. He also holds an ADB in Economics from the University of Denver.

Bagher joined the Carey Business School (formerly known as SPSBE) at Johns Hopkins University, where he mainly taught graduate courses in international and strategic marketing. After seven years, in 2013, he transitioned to the University of Maryland's Smith School of Business and later joined the School of Public Policy's Executive Programs. With his multidisciplinary academic background, he has been teaching a diverse range of graduate courses. In recognition of his contributions, he was awarded "Most Valuable Professor" at the University of Maryland in 2018.

Bagher has also consulted for and conducted seminars at several global organizations, including the Global Division of General Motors and Westinghouse. Among his accomplishments, for eight years, he also served as a commissioner in the State of Maryland.

Bagher is a world traveler who has lived in several countries in the Middle East and Western Europe, as well as in the United States and Canada. He is multilingual with an in-depth appreciation and understanding of multicultural settings. He is the author of *Global Communications and Misunderstandings: An Exploratory Study of Interpersonal Relationships, Management, Business Negotiations, and Promotional Marketing in Diverse Cultural Settings* (2009). He has also published another book, *Cross-Cultural Communication with Success: An Interpersonal and Organizational Perspective in a Changing World* (2013).

TABLE OF CONTENTS

PREFACE

Since my teenage years, I have had the opportunity to visit several countries and immerse myself in their cultures. I have been fascinated by the variety of languages, customs, and the ways people interact in both social and professional settings. For example, I observed that in some cultures, people dine quickly and leave shortly after finishing their meals, while in others, they spend the entire evening eating and socializing.

Globalization and the interconnectedness of cultures are more significant than ever. A clear example of this is the rising number of students pursuing education abroad. Twenty years ago, when I taught graduate marketing courses at Johns Hopkins University, nearly all my students were American. Today, at the University of Maryland, where I currently teach, approximately half of my students are international.

Throughout my teaching, consulting, and presentations, I have shared numerous first-hand cases of misunderstanding that occurred during negotiations and other interactions in multicultural settings. Shortly before the publication of this book, a graduate student in one of my business and negotiation courses reflected on his learning experience and said, "The focus on innovative tactics of modern negotiation, rather than just book knowledge, is highly relevant in today's environment and everywhere in the world."

Many have encouraged me to write a book on the subject. The idea slowly took shape in my mind, and finally, this book was born.

INTRODUCTION

Our reliance on interpersonal and corporate communication is an increasingly fast-paced trend. One reason for this trend is the technological advancements in communication, such as the Internet and teleconferencing, which facilitate sending and receiving messages. The other reason is the need for more communication, brought on by economic integrations, outsourcing, and the expansion of world trade, mainly because of the markets, to name a few.

Expectedly, more communication leads the way to misunderstanding or to being misunderstood. I am writing this book considering how a simple misunderstanding could create severe consequences. Misunderstanding has no boundaries; for instance, it can occur between friends, co-workers, and business negotiators. As I will explain, it is more apparent in international settings because of the diversity of customs, protocols, perceptions, and languages.

This book aims to raise awareness of various situations and types of misunderstanding that can occur both within and between cultures, particularly in interpersonal communications, management, marketing, and negotiations. To address this, I conclude with a set of guidelines designed to minimize misunderstandings. My goal is to promote a shared understanding among all individuals in our culturally diverse environments.

I use the term "misunderstanding" in a broad sense, encompassing both intentional and unintentional ambiguity, as well as the dissemination of misleading information. Another important note to the readers is that a range of cultures and customs are reviewed merely on a comparative basis with no intention of being judgmental.

CHAPTER ONE

~

THE NATURE, PURPOSE, AND PROCESS OF COMMUNICATION

Yu, an exchange student from China, came to the United States to pursue her education at one of the most well-known universities on the East Coast. Her objective was to earn a B.S. degree in Business Administration. In one of the required courses in which she was enrolled, the instructor assigned 20 out of 100 points for class participation toward the final grade.

Yu had demonstrated excellent work on her exams and quizzes in class, but she fell short in class participation and in asking questions. It appeared to the instructor that she had a strong background in mathematics; therefore, she didn't take the course seriously enough to engage in class discussions. Subsequently, she received a low mark in this part of the evaluation, which affected her final grade.

Her minimal class participation, however, was not because of a lack of interest in this class; rather, it was because of two notable reasons. First, Yu was fluent in the English language, but she had an accent, which made her feel uncomfortable speaking in front of others in class. Second, in Chinese culture, a high level of respect is placed on the elderly and those of higher authority. With this consideration, when instructions or assignments are given by the teacher, students typically follow them, instead of questioning them. In short, Yu received a lower final grade because she wanted to recognize and respect the authority of her professor. This is a case of simple misunderstanding, where behavior with good intentions is interpreted negatively.

In another case related to teaching and learning in multicultural settings, Sofia, an international student, stated that at the beginning of her first graduate class, the professor requested to be called by his nickname "Dick." Sofia was uneasy about using such informality with her professor. She pointed out that using the first name or nickname in her culture is reserved for friends and family. Sofia added that she expects formality in a classroom setting and wants to respect the authority of her professor. While Sofia wanted to follow formal protocol, her professor thought she was not pleased with the course and wanted to keep her distance from him.

Speaking of classrooms, in some schooling systems or cultures, it is customary for students to stand up when their instructor enters the classroom. The professor then gives the students permission to sit down. In my senior year at Boulder High School, during my math class, there was a student who stood up while others were seated in support of the instructor. The instructor could not understand why this student stood in the middle of the classroom until I had a chance to explain.

As another case of misunderstanding in the classroom, when I was an undergraduate student, I felt uncomfortable as my professor sat behind me to listen to students' presentations. For me, it was impolite to show my back to a professor. In these instances, I would turn my chair sideways. Some of my professors could not figure out my repositioning. Today, I see that some of my students are doing the same for me. And I simply thank them.

Such confusion has had an impact on the educational landscape across cultures, and yet sufficient attention has not been given to this issue. The breakdown of verbal and non-verbal communication is not limited to the teaching and learning environment, as it touches many aspects of human lives, as we shall see in this and the following chapters.

In some of the upcoming chapters, we will use the terms Low-Context Cultures (LCC) and High-Context Cultures (HCC), as introduced by Edward T. Hall in his renowned book, *Beyond Cultures*.[1] The distinction between the two is that in the LCC cultures, the meaning of a message is embedded in the words themselves, which means the "what" has been said. In the HCC, on the other hand, the meaning of a message largely depends on "how" the message was conveyed. Also, non-verbal cues such as tone of voice, facial expressions, and body gestures are parts of communication that are based on interpretation. As you can imagine, HCC is more complex than LCC, but understanding context often helps to save face in interpersonal dialogue. Some of the LCC countries are Sweden, Germany, the United States, and Switzerland. Spain, Japan, Ethiopia, and Pakistan mostly fall in the HCC countries. The terms Low Context Cultures and High Context Cultures will be used interchangeably with explicit and implicit communication.

The Three Perspectives of Communication

It is difficult, if not impossible, to quantify the rate of growth in human communication. However, the following three perspectives display the enormity of communication: national, organizational, and interpersonal.

Individual Perspective

Modern and technologically advanced modes of transportation, such as jetliners and high-speed trains, have remarkably increased global communication among individuals. Also, we can look at the overall rate of increase in per capita income worldwide as another condition for the expansion of travel. There are several reasons for people to travel from one country to another, for example, to explore investment prospects in emerging markets. Another driving force is to pursue higher education in a selected field of study and to pursue career opportunities. Another reason that people travel to other countries is to fulfill organizational missions. Individuals travel across national borders to acquire more knowledge about other cultures and customs or simply travel for excitement and pleasure.

Organizational Perspective

Increasing numbers of organizations that have been faced with the pressure of intra-industry competition are taking the initiative by going to other countries to seek new markets for their goods and services. These corporations select one or more types of entry in foreign markets, including exports, franchising, management contracts, contract manufacturing, turnkey operation, or strategic alliances. For instance, Kodak Corporation entered Japan's market through a fully owned subsidiary, while Japanese Fujifilm entered the U.S. market. Twix Cookie Bar, with the assistance of Grey Worldwide advertising agency, began its global expansion. Dell Computer, with its "just in time" approach, holds no inventory and builds its products based on consumers' orders worldwide.

Another reason for going international is to take advantage of certain opportunities that might not be available domestically. These include the low cost of production, less restrictive laws and regulations for companies' operations, and tax incentives that are offered by some developing countries to attract foreign investments. *The Wall Street Journal* reports on AON plc, which moved to England. David Prosperi, a spokesperson for the corporation, stated, "We want to be closer to where our clients are." This report also reveals that "Since 2009, at least 10 U.S. public companies have moved their incorporation address abroad or announced plans to do so.[2]

A pertinent point is the remarkable growth in foreign direct investment (FDI). In 1985, the FDI amounted to 57 billion dollars. In the year 2023, FDI rose to 1.364 trillion dollars with the nominal (not adjusted for the rate of inflation) average yearly rate of growth of 47%.[3] The expansion of emerging markets such as China, India, South Korea, South Africa, and Brazil seems to suggest that corporate involvement in the international arena will continue to grow on a long-term basis, which will be an indication of the growing trend of communication.[4]

In domestic and global organizations, three directions of communication are subject to misunderstanding. Downward communication signifies communication from a manager or superior to an employee. It is frequently used for the purpose of giving instructions, assignments, or performance evaluations. The next is upward communication, which refers to communication initiated by employees to superiors as a means to report their work progress, ask for guidance, or share any conflicts or problems that may affect the completion of their assigned tasks. Aside from upward and downward communication, there is lateral communication through which managers of the same hierarchical level communicate with each other mainly for the purpose of collaboration and coordination of workflow and resources.

Furthermore, the top manager communicates with the board of directors on a periodic basis to report overall organizational standing and performance and to receive recommendations. It should be mentioned that communicating with the stakeholders is considered a high priority for the top management. This includes communication with the entities, such as the community, government, and stockholders, which have a certain level of concern or interest regarding the organization.

National Perspective

Clusters of countries in a given region, commonly known as regional economic integrations, have been formed to minimize or eliminate trade barriers such as tariffs, quotas, or other similar measures among the member countries. The major purposes of economic integration are to promote economic cooperation and a higher level of competitiveness in the world market. A basic form of such integration is the Free Trade Area (FTA), such as the North American Free Trade Agreement (NAFTA), which comprises Canada, the United States, and Mexico. The

European Free Trade Association (EFTA) also functions under the FTA agreement and consists of Iceland, Liechtenstein, Norway, and Switzerland. (In this form of integration, there is generally free trade among the member countries. However, each member sets its trade policies toward non-member countries. As a result, regional economic integrations have prompted a surge in communication among countries.

Expansion of Communication

The development of artificial intelligence (AI) has played a crucial role in human lives in many ways.

As I was crossing the street, I twisted my foot. I sought treatment from a nearby physiotherapist for a few sessions. At the beginning of the first session, the therapist spent about 10 minutes asking me questions about how and when the injury occurred. After that, he mentioned needing a few minutes to consult about my injury. At one point, I realized that he was talking without receiving any response from anyone. When he came back, I asked him about it, and he smiled and said, "I was not talking to anyone; I was talking to my computer for advice."

I was invited to a birthday event at a Japanese restaurant where I saw some "real" robots. They were able to maneuver around anyone or obstacles in their way. The robot servers were about five feet tall with happy faces and shiny eyes. Their main tasks were to carry ordered food and stop at the assigned tables for delivery.

Not long ago, I visited the beautiful city of San Francisco, where I experienced my first ride in a driverless taxi, Waymo. It was thrilling to see how it obeyed the traffic lights and skillfully maneuvered in busy traffic. This unexpected experience offered me a glimpse into the future of how transportation will interact with its environment.

Elsewhere, in Norway, engineers have been developing robots that serve as housekeepers, showcasing yet another exciting advancement in the field of robotics. These "Norwegian robots" can answer the phone, clean the house, and even wash the dishes. These cutting-edge technologies all sound like something out of a science fiction movie, but they're real—and they're unfolding right before our eyes.

Technology is constantly transforming the way we live, to the extent that it has notably overshadowed humanity. Albert Einstein once said, and I quote, that "It has become appallingly obvious that our technology has exceeded our humanity." AI has had a significant impact on human life since it emerged in the early 1950s. Its influence is widespread across various sectors today, including environmental conservation, robotic surgery, finance, banking, and notably, human communication. Some specific benefits of AI related to communication are as follows:

- Calling a company's AI assistant to schedule a job interview.
- An AI-powered assistant can efficiently answer your questions by engaging in a dialogue with you.
- When someone contacts a financial company, an AI system prompts the caller to repeat a few sentences to verify their identity through voice recognition.

AI, however, has its limitations. For instance, it fails to recognize the emotions of the person with whom it communicates. It also lacks an understanding of communication effectiveness in cross-cultural environments. Thus, relying heavily on AI for communication could lead to a loss of human connection.

Recent technological advances in communication include ChatGPT. A report from Google Chrome on September 24, 2024, highlights that ChatGPT has over 100 million users daily. "Chat is a common descriptor for conversational interfaces, and 'GPT' refers specifically to a type of transformer model developed by OpenAI. The combination of these terms does not create a unique identifier but rather describes a category of AI models used for conversational purposes."

The benefits of ChatGPT are endless. For example, it can,

- Translate a letter from one language to another,
- Compose music or poetry,
- Give the recipe for a specific Italian food,
- Rewrite a letter,
- Generate ideas and solve mathematical problems.

In addition to such expansion, there have been impressive advances in telecommunication. I remember that about thirty years ago, calling overseas was often an annoying experience. The caller had to contact the telephone company, requesting to speak with an overseas operator. The overseas operator would collect necessary information from the caller, including the phone number of the other party overseas. Later that day, the operator would have contacted the caller, stating that the party was on the line. If there was a disconnection, which was not unusual, the caller had to go through the same process again. Now, we can dial directly to almost anywhere in the world, even with our cell phones.

Rotary telephones, typewriters, telegraphs, telexes, and even facsimile machines have given way to exponential innovations in communication technology. Social media platforms, blogs, video conferencing, email, the internet, text messages, and podcasts are among the advanced means of communication.

Advancements in communication technology also allow you to communicate with your automobile. You can command your automobile to find an address or a restaurant. More remarkably, you can command your automobile to find a parking space and to park itself. Moreover, if a driver becomes drowsy or sleepy, the car can sense the condition and send a voice message to the driver. The steering wheel, in the meantime, begins to vibrate to alert the driver.

The need for communication on national, organizational, and personal levels, along with the advances in more efficient and effective means of communication, has dramatically increased human contact. Concurrent with these developments, there has been a growing trend in misunderstanding, particularly when communication occurs among people with different languages, dialects, and customs.

How Do We Communicate?

A typical communication process consists of several distinct but highly interdependent steps, which are as follows:

The Initial Communicator is someone with a need or preference to communicate with another party. The initiator converts their intended thoughts and feelings into a message through a process known as encoding. The message is then conveyed to the other party through a channel such as e-mail or communication.

The receiver is the party who decodes the received message (who understands the message). Subsequently, the receiver of the message sends a response back to the initial communicator. The response, for example, could be:

"I agree, and I will do it..."

"I understand what you are saying, but I don't agree with it ..." or

"I am not sure what you are telling me...."

Such responses may prompt the initial communicator to compose and send another message. However, the receiver of a message may refuse to give any type of response to the initial communicator. The answer is likely to be no because no response is a response (feedback) in itself, particularly in face-to-face communication.

Barriers consist of any interference that impedes or compromises the effectiveness of communication.

Some of the most commonly cited barriers are:

- **Noise,** such as in conversations that take place near a busy intersection in the middle of town.

- **Distractive behavior** refers to any conduct that prevents concentration. An example is when a lecturer pounds on the podium with a pen or keeps pacing the classroom in a way that prevents students from focusing on what has been presented.

- **Semantics** is another potential barrier to effective communication. It refers to more than one meaning or interpretation of a given word or sentence. For example, "This outfit is so beautiful I could die for it."

- **Accent** as a barrier to communication is often noticed in diverse cultural settings.

I remember a miscommunication I observed at the Montgomery Mall in Bethesda, Maryland. A customer approached a sales associate at the counter and asked him for "Sears." The associate politely gave the directions to the Sears department store in the mall. The customer interrupted him and said, "I am not asking for the Sears store, but I am asking for sears." At that time, we were not sure of the man's intention. He said to the associate, "You know, I am looking for the drapes." Apparently, the customer wanted "sheers," but because of his accent, it was difficult for him to pronounce the sound "sh."

In some cultures, the term "excuse me" is pronounced "escosme," which sounds like "It kills me." Also, the word "thinking" may sound like "sinking."

Here's another example: A woman, while shopping at a local supermarket, saw the husband of one of her friends, who was under medical treatment for over a year. The woman asked her husband about his wife. The husband, with his heavy accent, replied, "She was finally cured by the doctor..." The woman, with great disbelief, expressed her condolences as she thought the husband was saying that the doctor killed her friend. This incident seemed to cause considerable embarrassment for the woman.

Why Do We Communicate?

We communicate for a variety of reasons. From a broad perspective, we rely on interpersonal communication to facilitate socialization as well as to perform tasks and functions. These are discussed in some detail below.

Social Satisfier and Health Promoter

Imagine that Jill just entered her newly rented apartment and must wait a few hours for the new furniture to be delivered. The place is empty, with no telephone, television, radio, or other means of communication. Or suppose that Donald wanted to be the first in line to enter a bank to see a loan officer. He arrived at the bank quite early and had to wait in the hallway for the bank to open.

These two individuals may have something in common. They may keep looking at their watches to see how time is dragging itself from one minute to another. That would be an annoying and unpleasant experience for them.

In one of my recent graduate classes, the topic discussed was employment satisfaction. One of the students, Bill, stated his dissatisfaction with his present job to the point that he was seeking work with another organization. Several students probed the cause of his dissatisfaction: Inconvenient hours? Not enough working space? Unreasonable expectations? Long drive to commute? Low pay? Many deadlines to meet? The answer was "no" to all of the above. Bill was working for a government agency where there was almost nothing for him to do. Every week, he had to sign off on similar or repetitive reports, and hardly any human interaction occurred during his working hours.

One of our basic needs is to socialize.[5] To be deprived of it causes life to be dull, boring, and uninspiring. This is where interpersonal communication comes to the rescue, as it acts as a bridge between our social needs and satisfaction.

Through socialization, we are able to share our feelings, experiences, intentions, and knowledge. Additionally, it is an opportunity to monitor the way we relate to others and make appropriate adjustments as needed. This reminds me of an old saga, which is worth mentioning here.

There was a man named Hakim, who was a role model for many because of his manner, courtesy, and the way he cared for others. Someone who was very impressed by Hakim could not keep himself from asking him a question. He asked Hakim: "How did you learn to become so well-mannered, courteous, and kind?"

Hakim paused and then responded, "It was simple, I learned it from those who were not very well-mannered, courteous, and kind..."

Health Promoters

In addition, the importance of touching and human contact is more serious than one might imagine. In the early part of the twentieth century, many babies died of a disease known as marasmus, meaning "wasting away" in Greek. This was a noticeable problem in many foundling establishments and hospitals in the United States. An investigation concluded that there were no cases of malnutrition or insufficient medical care, but the babies were deprived of "mothering." They were not given enough love and attention, such as holding the babies and carrying them around. In one of the hospitals, this practice was applied and resulted in a significant drop in the infant mortality rate.[6]

Customary Communication

There are many instances where people respond to a message without consciously thinking about it. For example, when someone checks in at their local gym and the front desk associate, as a good gesture, says, "Have a good workout."

The customer might reply, "Thank you, you too," without realizing that the associate is working. This demonstrates a disconnect between the sender and the receiver of a message.

Intellectual Competence

Occasionally, I have come across a question of concern from my students. They want to know what benefits come with learning subjects, such as mathematical calculations or statistical formulations that they will probably never see or use again. My response is that, at the very least, they are exercises for the mind.

For example, class and group discussions on such topics will enhance our reasoning ability and learning experience. Such exercises will help us with our comprehension and problem-solving abilities. I continue to say that it is like the fact that people who perform physical exercise over time are more likely to have stronger and fitter bodies than those who do not. At Michigan University, Oscar Ybarra, a professor of psychology, and his team conducted an interesting and extensive study. The outcome of their study suggests that socialization and discussions help to enhance "mental function."[7]

Confusions about the Time and Date

Different cultures or regions have varying understandings of time and dates. In the Middle East, the 24-hour clock, commonly known as military time, is used, especially in formal settings. This means that 2 PM is referred to as 14, 6 PM as 18, 10 PM as 22, and 12 PM as 24 o'clock.

Another source of persistent confusion is the way dates are written. Dates typically begin with the day, then the month, and finally the year. However, in the United States and some other countries, the month is written before the day. This variation has led to misunderstanding in many situations, such as booking a trip, date arrangements for international business negotiations, and other formal meetings.

Still, another source of confusion is how we assign evening or night to a range of times. Recently, I visited the charming city of Barcelona. During my short stay, there was the grand opening of a clothing store, and you needed to make an appointment to visit the store. This was my conversation with one of the staff at the door of the store.

Me: When is the earliest time I can visit the store?

Staff: At seven.

Me: Great, thank you. See you tonight.

Staff: ...We are closed tonight.

Me: Then when can I come?

Staff: At 7 pm, when we have an opening for you.

Me: Awesome, I will be here tonight.

Staff: We are not open tonight

Upon realizing the confusion, I asked, "When are you open?"

Staff: 9 AM to 8 PM.

Me: Great, so I will visit your store tonight.

Both of us laughed as we concurrently realized where the confusion stemmed from. For the Spanish, tonight begins at around 9 PM and not earlier.

Another Incident of Confusion

A couple, after nearly thirty years of marriage, had a serious argument and decided to sleep separately, in two different bedrooms located on the same floor of their house. Their daughter, Monica, along with her small dog, Bodie, stayed in the parents' home for a weekend. At night, Bodie, who always sleeps with Monica, sleeps in the hallway between the two bedrooms of the couple.

The next day, Monica sent a text message to her sister Kathy, informing her that Bodie had slept between their parents the previous night. The next day, Kathy visited their parents with a bottle of champagne to celebrate their renewed peaceful relationship.

Monica, in her text message, meant to say that Bodie slept in the hallway "between" the two bedrooms of her parents, while Kathy thought her parents were sleeping in the same bed and Bodie was between them.

A Moment of Embarrassment

In preparation for the winter season, I went to a large shoe store to buy a warm pair of boots. While trying on a few boots, I asked a woman who was passing by to help me with the quality and size of the boots. She spent about 10 minutes helping me find my favorite pair of boots. I thanked her, and she walked away.

I went to the cashier to pay, and while I was waiting in line, I saw the woman who had helped me was in line ahead of me. That's when I noticed she was a customer and not a store associate.

After we both paid for our purchases, I went to her to thank her again and apologize for my oversight. She smiled and said, "I knew you thought I worked here from the start. That's perfectly fine—I'm glad I could help."

Disconnect: A Matter of Protocol

Communication in diverse cultural settings assigns different meanings to interpersonal protocols or the norm of unwritten rules in dialogue, which I witnessed in the following situations.

In a family and friends gathering, the host's daughter was serving tea to the guests who had just joined. It was customary that the guest would not accept a cup of tea unless the host insisted. After a few guests had a cup of tea, when it was offered to the next host, she didn't go through the expected protocol of rejecting the cup of tea at first, instead as a compliment to the host, she said "Thank you so much...., I love it...," and as a courtesy to the host she picked-up the cup.

Later, the host's daughter commented to her mother that one of the guests had bad manners, and it looked like she had never had a cup of tea before, as she almost grabbed the cup out of my hand.

There was another incident that I was a part of. Henry is a friend of mine whose brother-in-law, Thomas, owns a major jewelry store. I asked Henry if I could see Thomas for any recommendations for buying a gift. Enthusiastically, Henry told him that my friend was coming to see him and that they should make sure he received the best service.

The next day, I went to the jewelry store with the help of Henry's brother-in-law and one of his sales associates. I bought what I wanted. Later that afternoon, Henry asked me about my contact with his brother-in-law. I precisely told him about my shopping experience. They were polite and courteous, but somewhat indifferent. Henry, who mainly relies on implicit communication, misunderstood my remark about their lack of enthusiasm — even though he had recommended them and is an old friend. Later, I found there was an argument between Henry and his brother-in-law, and friction that lasted for some time.

Handle It with Care

A message can be changed, added to, or deleted before its transmission, but once it is sent and decoded by the receiver, it is too late to erase it. Therefore, the message should be handled with care; otherwise, it may end up with unwanted consequences. According to a Chinese proverb, "We get sick from what we put in our mouths, but we get injured by what comes out of our mouths."[8]

The following is a story of a lumberjack and a lion that demonstrates this consequence. Once upon a time, deep in a forest, there was a lumberjack who had a lion friend. One day, while walking in the forest, he saw his lion friend and decided to invite him to his home for supper. The lion gladly accepted the lumberjack's invitation.

That evening, at the dinner table, the lumberjack was annoyed by the way the lion was gulping the food. In the middle of supper, the lumberjack couldn't keep himself from making a provocative remark about the lion's table manners. The lion paused and then asked the man to pick up his axe and hit him on the head. The confused man, with a quivering voice, responded, "But, why?"

The lion threatened the man's life if he didn't follow the order. Reluctantly, out of fear for his life, the lumberjack followed the lion's order by hitting the lion's head with the axe. The lion didn't say a word and walked away with a bleeding head.

Several years passed until one day, the lumberjack and the lion met each other eye to eye. The man was excited to see the lion, but still remembered the incident of that evening. After the usual greeting, the lumberjack, with hesitancy, asked the lion about his injury. The lion said, "First, let's see if you can find the spot where you hit me." The man looked at the lion's head very closely but could not see any scars.

The lion then declared rather sadly, "Although there is no trace of injury or pain from your axe, the pain of your words of humiliation is still with me, as your words were sharper than the edge of your iron axe."

What Is Ahead?

Human interactions occur in various settings and situations, including social gatherings, international business negotiations, job interviews, and marketing and purchasing decisions, among others. In examining these instances, we will explore the numerous misunderstandings and ambiguities related to verbal and non-verbal communication within and across different cultures. Also, they provide potential guidelines for more effective communication.

Communication of some sort is present in every aspect of our lives, and therefore, it leaves much potential for misunderstanding. With all good intentions between the communicators, misunderstanding and ambiguity can occur, particularly in international settings. This is because of a multitude of languages, customs, and cultural backgrounds. In the following chapters, I will differentiate between verbal and non-verbal communication and discuss how each could lead to misunderstanding if they are not handled with care.

Misunderstanding will be elaborated in several domains, which include interpersonal, organizational management, transportation, international marketing and promotional strategies, and intercultural business negotiations. Furthermore, a set of general guidelines will be given to enhance effective communication within and between cultures.

ENDNOTES

1. Edward T. Hall. *Beyond Culture* (Garden City, NY: Anchor Press, 1976).

2. John D. McKinnon and Scott Thurm, *The Wall Street Journal*, "U.S. Firms Move Abroad: Despite '04 Law, Companies Reincorporate Overseas, Saving Big Sum on Taxes", August 29, 2012, p. B1.

3. World Bank, *World Development Indicators database*, http://www.worldbank.org/query

4. Economist Intelligence Unit, *World Investment and the Challenge of Political Risk, written with the Columbia Program on Internation al Investment,* 2007, p. 6.

5. See Abraham H. Maslow, "A Theory of Human Motivation," *Psychological Review, 50, 1943, pp.370-396.* This theory provides a detailed explanation and hierarchy of human needs. Maslow's hierarchy of needs is notably popular and can be found in many textbooks of various fields, including management, organizational behavior, psychology, sociology, marketing, consumer behavior, and advertising.

6. Ashley Montagu, *Touching: The Human Significance of the Skin* (New York: Harper &Row, 1972), p. 93. in Ronald B. Adler and George Rodman, *Understanding Human*

Communication *(*New York: CBS College Publishing, 1982), p.121.

7. Oscar Ybarra, "Idle Chatter? Hardly," *Los Angeles Times*, November 5, 2007, Part F. p.2.

8. Roger E. Axtell, *The Do's and Taboos of International Trade: a Small Business Primer,* Revised ed. (New York: John Wiley & Sons, 1994), p. 216.

RECOMMENDED READING

Ashley Montagu. *Touching: The Human Significance of the Skin*. New York: Columbia University Press, 1971.

Lillian H. Chaney and Jeanette S. Martin. *Intercultural Business Communication*. Upper Saddle River, NJ: Prentice Hall, 2000.

Paul Watzlawick, Janet H. Beavin, and Don D. Jackson. *Pragmatics of Human Communication*. New York: W.W. Norton, 1967.

Rudolph F. Verderber. *Communicate*. Belmont, CA: Wadsworth, 1993.

Stanley Schachter. *The Psychology of Affiliation: Experimental Studies of the Sources of Gregariousness*. Stanford University Press: Stanford, 1968.

D. Nettle, "The evolution of personality variation in humans," *American Psychologist*, 2006, 61, 6522-6531.

B. M. Kitayyama and M. Karasawa, "Cultural affordance and emotional experience, *Journal of Personality & Social Psychology*, 2008, 95, 739756.

N. Alder, *International Dimensions of Psychological Behavior*, 4th ed. Mason, OH: South-Western, 2002.

CHAPTER TWO

~

VERBAL AND NON-VERBAL COMMUNICATION

The purpose of this chapter is to examine the concept of understanding or lack of it and to differentiate between explicit, also known as Low Context Cultures, LCC, and implicit, High Context Cultures, HCC, communication by explaining how the crossroads between them tend to create ambiguity and communication breakdown. Furthermore, this chapter discusses the many forms of verbal and non-verbal communication and their potential for misunderstandings, particularly in diverse cultural settings. Understanding and Its Related Categories

Understanding

Suppose a manager gives one of the employees an assignment with a designated due date. The job is done accordingly and submitted to the manager on time. This indicates that the employee received the message as intended by the manager. Clear understandings between the communicators are commonly known as effective communication.

Misunderstanding

Misunderstanding takes place when there is a discrepancy between the content of a message that is sent and its interpretation by the receiver. Misunderstanding is the source of many unwanted outcomes in interpersonal interactions. It can damage friendships and family relationships and derail business negotiations. Misunderstandings can even result in the loss of human lives, as will be shown later in this chapter.

There was a recent case caused by a misunderstanding that was brought before a small claims court judge. A buyer of household furniture (plaintiff) claimed that the salesperson (defendant) promised to let her have a sofa for free after buying the whole living room set. The salesperson stressed that while they were negotiating the price of a chair, he said to the buyer that she could have the sofa at the same price, meaning the same price as the chair, not one price for both items. The judge determined that this was a case of misunderstanding. He ruled that the buyer had to either pay the same price for the sofa as she did for the chair or return the sofa to the seller.

Imitate Understanding

There are situations in which the receiver of a message does not fully understand what is being communicated but prefers to demonstrate understanding anyway. For example, a manager gives a procedural instruction to a group of employees and asks if anyone needs further explanation. One employee did not understand the instructions but did not ask for further clarification. It could have been because he or she was uncomfortable asking questions when presumably others did understand. Another example is when a student's attention is on a personal matter, but he or she appears attentive during a lecture.

Imitate Not Understanding

In many cases, the receiver of a message pretends to lack understanding of what is being said. For example, in the case of a dispute, one person may say to the other, "I don't understand what you are talking about," when indeed the message is fully understood. Asking for the repetition of the same message allows the recipient to formulate a more compelling response.

One of my friends, Alfred, shared this experience with me. He said that one of his relatives, who lives overseas, once called him requesting to borrow $2,500.00, explaining the urgency of the matter. The relative promised to pay back the sum within one month. Alfred hesitantly agreed to his relative's request and sent the money. Alfred waited for about six weeks without hearing from the borrower. Since then, my friend has reached his relative on the phone several times. He pointed out that when he talked about anything but the borrowed money, they had a perfect phone connection. However, the moment he started asking him for the $2,500, his relative suddenly began to experience a very bad phone connection with him and could not understand what was being said.

There are many forms of misunderstanding, as we will review in the upcoming chapters. However, the focus here is on misunderstandings relevant to the study of verbal explicit-direct and verbal implicit-indirect interpersonal communication.

A Gentle Comment

Mr. F. is an active member of a professional association and usually shows up to the meetings wearing the latest style suits and designer ties. At one of the meetings, Mr. F. arrived a few minutes late in an uncommonly casual outfit. Another member, Mr. B., as an ice-breaking device, commented, "What happened to your tie? You forgot to wear it?" The misunderstanding was that Mr. F. thought this comment in the presence of others was a way to remind him that he needed to have a professional look for all meetings. Mr. F. then expected some type of reaction.

At the next meeting, Mr. F. was unfriendly toward Mr. B. During that meeting, in a subtle manner, Mr. F. made remarks on the lack of validity of some of the points Mr. B. was making. Mr. B., unaware of the motive for this member's behavior, decided to react as well. This misunderstanding manifested itself in an action-reaction loop that affected their professional relationship. Therefore, it is crucial to be cognizant of the multiple dimensions of communication breakdown as a result of verbal and non-verbal communication. Equally important is to avoid falling into the loop of action-reaction in such a way that it deepens the existing misunderstanding in interpersonal communication.

Verbal Explicit, LCC, and Implicit, HCC Communication

Explicit communication is generally directed towards giving instructions and task accomplishment, with less concern focused on feelings and relationships. Implicit communication, on the other hand, is indirect, having more concern about upholding good relationships. Many question the benefit of sending an indirect message.

First, if I send you an indirect message and you are able to decode the message the way I intended, then we are having clear and effective communication. Additionally, in many interpersonal relationships and negotiations, as well as in organizational management, indirect messages can serve the intended purpose while saving face and maintaining positive relationships.

Effective use of implicit and explicit communication is quite situational and is a function of many factors, some of which are indicated as follows.

- The cultural settings and individual attitudes, perceptions, and expectations through which interpersonal communication takes place,

- The organizational or corporate culture in which employees interact,

- One's comfort zone and habits of using direct and indirect communication,

- The level of understanding, friendship, and cooperation among the communicators,

- The nature and the content of the message that needs to be communicated,

- The urgency of communication, and

- The importance of saving face and maintaining harmony in interpersonal relationships.

Explicit or Implicit Communication is a matter of choice. The sender of a message is in charge of deciding whether to rely on explicit or implicit communication. The following are two examples that show both types of communication.

While I was a student at the University of Colorado, one of the emeritus professors, Dr. N., was diagnosed with cancer. A University administrator and I volunteered to drive Dr. N. once a week from Boulder to Denver for cancer treatments. One day, after the treatment was administered, the physician asked Dr. N. and me to wait in his office. I needed to be there to assist him in walking.

The physician reviewed some charts and documents, then informed Dr. N. that he had about two months left to live. Dr. N. seemed to have difficulty believing what he had just heard. He then turned his head toward me and asked me to repeat the physician's comment. Saddened by the news and with hesitancy, I started my euphemistic version, during which I was interrupted by the physician, who repeated his earlier pronouncement. Dr. N. was so distraught by the news that he almost fainted.

A few years back, in one of my business classes, I handed out the students' midterm exams that I had graded. At the end of the class period, one of my students came to me with her exam. Politely, she asked if I could further explain the answer to one of the questions on the exam. While looking at the question, I noticed that, inadvertently, I had not given her points for the correct answer to that specific question. Implicit communication directed my attention to the answer with the missing points.

Non-verbal Communication

As we shall see, non-verbal communication is a resourceful way to send or receive messages. Peter Drucker, who is known as the father of modern management, noted that "The most important thing in communication is to hear what isn't being said."[1]

Verbal communication is limited to spoken and written forms, but there are many types of non-verbal cues, including facial expressions, gestures, selection of color and style of clothing, overall physical appearance, handshakes, tone of voice, and manners, to name a few. Non-verbal communication has considerably more potential for misunderstandings.

In this section of the chapter, I will describe a few types of non-verbal communication as related to ambiguity and misinterpretations.

Facial Expression and Nodding

An important part of non-verbal communication is facial expression, which enriches verbal communication by signaling many messages, such as happiness, surprise, confusion, shame, fear, or frustration, to name a few.

Many instructors who teach asynchronous time-independent courses assert that because they are unable to see the facial reactions of their students while teaching, it is difficult to know which point should be repeated or reemphasized. In this regard, one of my colleagues who teaches mathematics courses online pointed out that the number of students who fail his online courses is noticeably higher than the failure rate in traditional classroom settings.

Another example of a facial expression is nodding, which often replaces or supports the word "yes" or "no." The interpretation of nodding is not the same among all cultures, so it may result in misunderstanding. In North America, vertical movement of the head commonly signifies "yes" or agreement with what has been conveyed. On the other hand, in some parts of India, a horizontal movement of the head is used to send similar messages.

Some years ago, I went to a casual Indian restaurant in Takoma Park, Maryland, for a carry-out lunch. When it was my turn to order, I asked for a dozen samosas. The restaurant was very busy, and it was sometimes hard to communicate with the person across the counter. I was asked if I wanted frozen samosas. In response, I relied on my non-verbal communication by moving my head horizontally, meaning "no," but it was understood as "yes." Later, I found that all of my samosas were frozen.

Many management, communication, and professional development training programs mention the importance of eye contact. However, it should be noted that its importance varies across cultural settings. In China, Japan, and many South American countries, eye contact is de-emphasized. A few years ago, the manager of a clothing store dismissed one of the sales associates.

His reasoning was that "He never wanted to make eye contact with me. I knew that he was hiding something from me, which made me very concerned and uncomfortable." Later on, through several casual conversations with the sales associate, the manager found that the sales associate who tried to avoid eye contact did it out of respect for his superior.

Fingers

Our fingers are a major source of wordless communication. They are usually used to show facts, whereas facial expressions mainly display feelings and emotions.

Each day, there may be many occasions in which we rely on our fingers as a reliable source to communicate with others. They are used to indicate a direction, such as showing the shortest distance on a map. Fingers are also used to indicate numerical value. Consider a crowded movie theater line, we might use our fingers to show the number of tickets we want to purchase.

Careful usage of fingers is important for minimizing misunderstandings, notably in multifaceted cultural settings. A server might ask a guest in a restaurant, "How is your food?" While eating, the guest might form a circle by connecting his thumb and index finger to indicate that the food is sumptuous. This formation of the circle, however, does not have the same meaning in every country. For example, it is a vulgar sign in Pakistan or Turkey.

In the United States, during the late 60s and early 70s, raising both the index and middle finger to create a "V" shape became a popular gesture, symbolizing peace and friendship.[2] Although this tends to have a somewhat universal meaning, in some countries it still translates into an offensive gesture.

Colorful Cultures

Colors are another significant means of unwritten and unspoken communication that we rely on. The following are a few illustrations of their uses.

Means of Guidance

When entering a hospital, often in front of the information desk, there are several lines on the floor, each with a distinct color that guides visitors to their desired unit, such as emergency or intensive care. Following a colored designated walkway to a specific unit is less confusing than looking at a map. There are more situations in which colors are used to indicate directions, such as in metro stations.

Another use of color is to facilitate the flow of traffic on the roads and minimize accidents. Traffic lights at intersections, yield signs, and railroad crossing signs are a few examples of color's importance.

Meaning and Interpretation of Colors

In terms of meaning and interpretation, colors are not immune to misunderstandings. In the United States, the color green symbolizes prosperity and growth, as well as concern for nature. For instance, the term "green marketing" denotes production and other marketing activities performed in an environmentally responsible manner. The interpretation of this color may not be the same across cultures. In this regard, let us consider the following multiple-choice questions.

1) In which country is the color green associated with danger and disease? _____.

   a) Guatemala

   b) Mali

   c) Malaysia

   d) Switzerland

2) In Western Europe, purple is the color of prestige and grandeur, but in various parts of _____, it symbolizes death or mourning.

   a) The Middle East

   b) The Far East

   c) Africa

   d) South America

3) In _____, avoid offering gifts with a white ribbon, as it is the color of death and mourning.

42

a) Japan

b) Bolivia

c) Finland

d) Italy

4) Yellow roses may symbolize sadness and despair in some parts of _____.

a) Western Europe

b) The Middle East

c) North America

d) Australia

5) Red is the color of joy and good luck in _____.

a) China

b) Pakistan

c) Turkey

d) Greece

6) Brown, tar-colored teeth in some parts of _____ are a sign of sophistication and wealth.

a) Australia

b) Zambia

c) Thailand

d) New Zealand

The answers to the above questions are: 1.c, 2.d, 3.a, 4.b, 5.a., and 6.c.

The selection of colors should be a matter of importance in international activities, notably in marketing mix strategies to avoid blunders and misunderstandings.

Let us also answer the following five questions relevant to non-verbal communication in international settings.

1) In which of the following countries are smiles among parties the least noticeable during business negotiations? _____ .

   a) Venezuela

   b) South Africa

   c) Russia

   d) Italy

2) In which of the following countries do negotiators tend to stand closest to one another? _____ .

   a) Switzerland

   b) Germany

   c) Norway

   d) Peru

3) During a dialogue, the movement of hands and arms are least and most noticeable respectively in _____ .

   a) Spain and Pakistan

   b) Chad and Turkey

   c) Japan and Italy

   d) None of the above

4) Respect for the authority of managers in a corporate setting is most noticeable in _____.

   a) The United States

   b) Canada

   c) Australia

   d) Pakistan

5) Touching one another among friends in social settings is more common in _____.

   a) Russia

   b) Switzerland

   c) Germany

   d) Nepal

The answers to the above questions are: 1.c., 2.d., 3.c., 4.d., and 5.d.

Final Notes

Non-verbal cues have a wider variation than verbal communication. Additionally, the extent of their usage and interpretations differ across nations. Non-verbal cues can stand alone as methods of conveying intended messages or can be complementary to verbal communication in face-to-face situations. Considering various scenarios as described above, it becomes clear how simple it is for misunderstandings to arise.

ENDNOTES

1. M. Peter F. Drucker, in an interview with Bill Moyer, A World of Ideas (New York: Doubled, 1989), P. 408.

2. It is based on the author's observation.

RECOMMENDED READING

Don Hellriegel and John W. Slocum, Jr. *Organizational Behavior*. Mason, OH: Thomson South-Western, 2007.

John J. Macionis. *Sociology*. Upper Saddle River, NJ: Pearson Prentice Hall, 2007.

Ronald B. Alder and George Rodman. *Understanding Human Communication*. Fort Worth, TX: Harcourt Brace College Publishers, 1994.

Tom D. Daniel and Barry K. Spiker. *Perspectives on Organizational Communication*. Madison, WI: WCB Brown and Benchmark, 1987.

William L. Gorden. *Communication: Personal and Public*. Sherman Oaks, CA: Alfred Publishing Company, 1978.

CHAPTER THREE

~

THE MANY FACES
OF
MISUNDERSTANDING

In this chapter, I will present cases of misunderstanding resulting from verbal and non-verbal communication. These cases will illuminate a range of outcomes and show the extent to which misunderstandings can be catastrophic. There will be some references to acronyms, jargon, and colloquialisms as potential sources of misunderstandings.

The chapter will include two personal cases of misunderstanding to describe how someone with good intentions can cause unwanted situations.

Finally, I will explain that not all misunderstandings are unintentional. As we shall see, there are situations in which someone creates a misunderstanding intentionally for one reason or another.

Unintentional Misunderstandings

In this section, several cases of unintentional misunderstandings will be illustrated, some of which are verbal and non-verbal concurrently. In these unintentional misunderstandings, you will find significant differences among conditions and outcomes. Two of these situations are the result of my own misunderstanding, which will be explained later in the chapter.

Don't Throw Away Those Matches!

The following case illustrates how a brief statement led to an inaccurate conclusion about another individual.

In a remote small town, Joe, the owner of a grocery store, wanted to borrow money to expand his business. Since there were no financial institutions available in that town, borrowers were dependent on a few individual lenders. Joe heard of a generous man who had helped several business owners with their financial needs. By a previous arrangement, Joe went to see the lender at his home. Right before ringing the bell, through the open windows, he heard the man telling someone, "Why are you wasting these few matches? Don't throw them away." Joe became hesitant to see the lender. After all, how generous could that man be if he was so concerned with a few matches? Despite his pessimism, Joe finally decided to go ahead and meet with the lender. This was an opportunity for Joe to explain

49

his need to borrow money for his grocery store. Shortly, an agreement was made between the two.

Before leaving, Joe hesitantly and curiously wanted to know how a generous man like the lender was also so frugal over a few matches. Joe finally asked the question. The lender, with a smile, replied, "I can see the misunderstanding caused by what I said about the matches and my willingness to help you out!" He continued by saying, "It is quite simple; if I were not a thrifty person, I would not have saved enough money to help others expand their businesses."

Misunderstanding the Term "As Usual"

Recently, the parents of one of my colleagues, Dr. H., came from overseas to visit their son in Virginia. During their stay with their son, they were given a calling card so they could call their extended family and friends in the United States. The parents also wanted to contact other friends and relatives overseas. Ms. H. asked her son whether they needed to use the calling card or whether they should call directly. Dr. H. said, "Simply dial as usual," meaning to use the calling card as she did before. However, Ms. H. thought "as usual" meant calling overseas by direct dialing.

A few weeks later, Dr. H. received the usual telephone bill, except this time it was unusually high. The monthly payment that normally totaled around $100.00 now amounted to almost $2,700.00. Dr. H., who thought that there must have been a mistake, at once contacted the telephone company and found that there had been many hours of conversation from his telephone number to other countries.

Luckily, Dr. H. explained the misunderstanding between himself and his parents regarding the term "as usual" and received a break on the bill.

A Case of Dry Cleaning

The wife of the CEO of an electronics corporation in Virginia wanted to send her expensive clothing and garments to the nearby, rather exclusive, dry cleaner. For this, she instructed one of the maids to call the dry cleaner to come to the house and pick up a few bags of clothing. The maid immediately called the store with the instructions.

In the meantime, a not-for-profit organization called the house and asked for donations. Another maid happened to answer the phone. The maid, who had a large amount of her own unwanted clothing, happily agreed to donate it. She informed the caller that she would put the clothing in a few bags and leave them in front of the house for pickup, but she completely forgot to do so.

The next day, the truck for the not-for-profit organization arrived at the house. Outside, there were a few bags of clothing meant for dry cleaning and not for donation, but were inadvertently picked up by the not-for-profit organization.

Several days later, a maid in the house called the dry cleaner to find out when the clothing would be ready and delivered to the house. The manager of the store said that they came to the house for the pickup, but there was nothing to pick up.

Pointing the Finger

One of my friends is a doctor of psychiatry and lives in Canada with his family. Recently, they spent their vacation in the United States, during which time they were invited to our home. His spouse had an experience concerning one of his psychiatric inpatients, which she shared with us.

One evening, while Mrs. N. and her husband were doing their grocery shopping, a middle-aged man smiled at her husband and walked toward them. Dr. N. then introduced the man to his wife. Mrs. N. thought he must have been one of her husband's colleagues, and as a result, she took a friendly approach to him. She said, "How are things going with you?" The man, a patient of Dr. N's, assumed that his doctor had already talked about him to Mrs. N. Therefore, the patient replied, "Thanks to your husband, I am feeling much better and have no more problems with the law." Mrs. N., who was taken by surprise, said, "Well, I am very happy to hear that." At that time, mistakenly, the patient was confident that his psychiatrist had spoken about him with his wife or maybe even with some others as well. Soon after, the patient complained to the hospital that his psychiatrist had failed to keep the confidentiality of his patients and requested that the hospital designate another psychiatrist for him.

International Driving

In the international arena, variations of norms, regulations, and laws pertinent to driving are sources of confusion.

In most countries, vehicles drive on the right-hand side of the road, including the United States and Germany. However, there are some exceptions, as driving is on the left-hand side in countries like England and Singapore. This is often a source of confusion and accidents. Here are two distinct rules of driving worth mentioning.

Recently, a pilot from an international airline spent a few days in a country where drivers paid little attention to obeying traffic rules.

One morning, while the pilot was riding in a taxi, the taxi driver and the pilot had a casual chat when the taxi driver noticed the passenger was a pilot. Out of curiosity, the taxi driver asked the passenger about his scariest moment in his career.

Without hesitation, the pilot replied, "The scariest moment of his life is right now, the way you drive and ignore the red lights."

With a smile, the taxi driver responded, "Dear pilot, stopping at the red light is not mandatory; the red traffic lights are only for those who wish to stop. They are allowed to do so."

During an ice-breaking session in one of my classes with mostly international students, I asked if anyone had experienced culture shock in the United States. One student mentioned that if you don't drive properly in the United States and don't stay in your lane, the police might assume that you have been drinking and stop you. He added that in his country, it's different because the roads are bumpy, so if you drive straight through the bumps, the police might stop you, suspecting that you've been drinking.

Which Way to Look?

In one of my graduate courses, we were discussing the challenges associated with non-verbal communication in international settings. One of these challenges was how the same behavior or signal could have different meanings because of cultural variations. In this regard, one of my students shared her own experience with us.

Linda was working for an international airline company when she met a young man from Peru, whom she later married. Now, they have a son named Mike who is six years old. Linda continued by saying that, like most Americans, she was accustomed to frequent eye contact with whomever she was communicating. She said that she was annoyed by her son, who would lean his head downward during their conversation, thus preventing eye contact. Linda then had to say, "Mike, I am not on the floor. Look at me when I am talking."

When her husband wanted to speak with Mike, it was another story. He was accustomed to having minimal eye contact in his conversations with others. He had already said several times to Mike that he should show some respect to his father by not looking at him.

Linda, furthermore, commented that at one time, both parents wanted to speak with Mike. As usual, she wanted him to make eye contact with her, and her husband wanted the opposite. Mike, who was confused and tired, in a witty way told them, "Why don't you two make up your mind as to what you want me to do: eye contact or no eye contact."

Misunderstanding and Disaster

In aviation history, there have been many cases of jetliner crashes caused by some simple misunderstanding that ended with irrevocable, catastrophic results. The following are two such cases.

Running Out of Fuel

On January 25, 1990, an Avianca Airlines Boeing 707 was en route to New York from Medellin, Colombia. While the jetliner circled in the air waiting for clearance from the control tower to land at Kennedy International Airport, the aircraft's fuel reached an alarmingly low level. The pilots informed the tower of their problem but failed to convey the gravity of their condition.

Shortly after this communication, the aircraft crashed, resulting in 73 deaths. After an investigation, "…the safety board concurred with the aviation agency's arguments that it was up to the pilots to declare an emergency explicitly under the circumstances." They should have reported an "emergency" for priority landing.[1]

From our previous discussions, it appears that the communication breakdown between the pilots and the controller was the result of direct and indirect communication. The pilots decoded the message in a more implicit manner to the controller, who was familiar with direct messages not requiring interpretation. The following is another case of a simple misunderstanding that claimed several hundred human lives.

Two Jumbo Jets Collided

Is it possible that a simple misunderstanding can lead to one of the worst disasters in aviation history, resulting in a huge loss of human lives? On March 27, 1977, Tenerife Airport in the Canary Islands was covered with heavy clouds, causing extremely poor visibility when a KLM 747 jumbo jet was en route to Amsterdam. A few seconds after the KLM aircraft had taken off, it slammed into the fuselage of a Pan Am 747 jumbo jet that was on the runway. The cockpit crew of the KLM aircraft attempted to prevent the collision, but the plane was unable to gain sufficient altitude to avoid the crash, resulting in the loss of over 587 lives.

A joint report by KLM and Pan American Airlines revealed that a major cause of the disaster was a communication misunderstanding between the control tower and the KLM cockpit crew. The report stated, "When the KLM co-pilot repeated the ATC (which stands for air traffic control) clearance, he ended with the words, 'We are now at takeoff.[2]

"The controller, who had not been asked for takeoff clearance, and consequently had not granted it, did not understand they were taking off. The okay from the tower, which preceded the 'stand by for takeoff' was likewise incorrect-although irrelevant in the case because takeoff had already started...."[3]

Communication in a multicultural environment can remind us that semantics is a barrier to effective communication. As noted above, to the KLM co-pilot, the term "We are now at takeoff" meant we are gaining speed on the runway to become airborne. To the tower controller, this term appeared to mean a request for permission to take off, which was followed by "okay..."

Fatal Error

Earlier, in chapter one, I referred to technological advancements that enable humans and machines to communicate with each other.

These connections are also prone to communication breakdowns, such as the following disaster, which occurred in late 1995.

An American airline Boeing 757 with 163 people onboard was en route from Miami to Cali, Colombia, when it crashed near the town of Buga, near the summit of El Deluvio, causing 159 deaths.

During the flight, the tower controller provided an optional shortcut route to the cockpit crew because the plane was delayed in leaving Miami. The crew agreed to the option, but they fell short in the necessary preparations.

"The report said that either the pilot or the co-pilot tried to reprogram the onboard computer using a radio beacon at an intermediate point, Razo, but erroneously entered only the letter "R," not the full name as required for that beacon. The letter "R" identifies "Romeo," another beacon on the same frequency but 132 miles northeast of Cali."[4]

Additionally, the pilot failed to double-check the data entered by the co-pilot, part of the mandated policy of American Airlines. [5]

In the cockpit, human errors take place in multiple forms. Stress, drowsiness, information overload, and insufficient training of the pilot and co-pilot to use more sophisticated onboard equipment are some of the problems. However, it appears that the most cited error is a communication breakdown between the flight crew and the tower controllers.

Such conditions call for more intercultural communication training programs for all parties involved to improve the efficiency and effectiveness of communications.

Same Culture, Different Understanding

A message can be encoded in a simple and clear way, but could reach the receiver without the same meaning. Divergent perceptions, experiences, and contexts are among the many sources of miscommunication.

For example, Gerald M. Goldhaber included the following in his book on communication. In a film on communication, a manager asked an employee for a "model job." Following the manager's request, the employee created a simulation of his electrical and mechanical work. The disenchanted manager declared, "I didn't ask for this!" The employee replied, "But boss, you asked me to produce a model job, and that's what I did!" The manager finally shouted, "Don't listen to what I say, listen to what I mean." [6]

The Gap Between the Encoded and the Decoded Messages

Such conditions occur not only in diverse cultural settings but also in a given cultural environment. Often, an individual composes a message by assuming that it precisely reflects that individual's thoughts and intentions. The receiver, however, may assign a different meaning to the received message, which ultimately creates misunderstandings and confusion.[7]

The following messages are from the letters on file at the San Antonio, Texas Veterans Administration:

"Both sides of my parents are poor, and I can't expect anything from them, as my mother has been in bed for one year with the same doctor, and won't change."

***

"I am annoyed to find out that you branded my child as illiterate. It is a dirty lie, as I married his father a week before he was born."

***

"You changed my little boy to a girl, does this make a difference?"

***

"In accordance with your instructions, I have given birth to twins in the enclosed envelope."

***

"My husband had his project cut off two weeks ago, and I haven't had any relief since."

Keeping these letters in mind, it is very important to be aware of sending messages that fail to transmit the intended meaning.

Ceremonial Proposition

One of the multinational corporations organized a welcoming event for its repatriates. The keynote speaker of the event was the vice president of the company, who encouraged the repatriates to ask questions. At the end of his presentation, many hands were raised. Oddly enough, it was evident that the speaker was reluctant to respond as he gave very short and closed-ended answers. Subsequently, after a few responses, no one wanted to pose questions.

This experience suggests that soliciting questions from the audience is generally expected of speakers. However, some speakers hope that no one will ask any questions, fearing the possibility of being put on the spot. In this case, "Ask any questions" really meant, "Don't ask any questions." In other words, for some, such an offering is simply ceremonial and should not be taken in a literal fashion.

The above scenario is not an isolated case. There are many cases in which a member of management makes statements solely as a matter of formality. They expect a gap between what they say and what should be done. An assistant professor of a private university once stated that in various meetings, the dean of the school and the chair of the department addressed the need to prevent grade inflation. However, lowering the standard for grading creates multiple side effects for the faculty, the department, and, in some cases, the university. An adjunct faculty member who does not

61

inflate grades is subject to low teaching evaluations from the students.

Subsequently, the adjunct with low marks from the students will not be invited to teach for the upcoming terms. Therefore, listening to the dean and the chair on this topic means losing a teaching position.

By lowering grade standards, there will be fewer students who fail, which poses additional concerns. Expectedly, the complaints of students, and in some cases those of parents, will increase, causing more headaches for the dean and the chair. Higher student failures lead to higher levels of student dropout, leading to a substantial financial loss for the institution. The assistant professor furthermore stressed the possibility of more cheating and plagiarism, which can pose further complications for the university as a whole.

Misinterpretation of a Compliment

Have you been in a situation where you wanted to compliment some of your associates on their superior performance and dedication, but your expression somehow turned out to be more like a criticism? Or, you simply wanted to wish someone well, but it was interpreted as an ill wish? It seems that this type of misunderstanding occurs more than expected, particularly among people of different cultures.

In many Asian countries, being "fat" is a sign of being healthy because being meager or slim indicates malnourishment and sickness. Furthermore, being "fat" is a sign of being wealthy because an individual doesn't need to work and can afford to eat a lot.

Newstrom and Davis stated that a movie director commented to Joe, who was playing in a scene, that "Joe, you are doing one hell of a job." The comment was interpreted as a criticism, which made Joe quite agitated.[8]

A teenager who grew up in Western culture and was studying abroad went home to stay with her parents for the summer vacation. While there, at one point, her grandmother wished her to become "fat." The teenage daughter became irritated and was astounded at the comment.

Colloquialisms, Jargons, and Acronyms

Colloquialisms, jargon, and acronyms are all major producers of misunderstandings, particularly in intercultural settings. Let us review some of them.

Colloquialism

This term refers to a set of words composed in such an order that they carry a figurative meaning for people of a common culture.

"He bought a lemon" refers to purchasing a car with many mechanical problems.

"She was born with a silver spoon in her mouth" means that she was born into a wealthy family.

In France, when someone says, "Je n'ai pas froid aux yeaux," it means, "I am not afraid." However, it literally translates in English to, "I do not have a cold in the eyes."

Jargons

Various occupational fields have their own jargon or specialized terminology. This is to facilitate and expedite their communication. Jargon can be ambiguous to those outside a specific field and can easily create miscommunication. For example, a governmental bureaucrat might say, "In this department, there is a lot of red tape." This means that in the department, there is an excessive amount of paperwork.

A financial broker might say, "This mutual fund is a no-load," which means the mutual fund has no sales charge. When someone says the market is "bearish," they are expressing pessimism about the market.

When a captain of a ship declares, "May Day," it means there is a distressing situation, an emergency.

The field of medicine has much jargon of its own. What do you think a "frequent flyer" is? If the answer is someone who travels by plane frequently, then the answer is correct. However, this term in the medical field has a different meaning. It refers to a patient who comes to the emergency room frequently for unnecessary reasons.

A physician once mentioned that she sometimes has a difficult time communicating with her patients. She stated that the medical term "hypertension" means high blood pressure. Thus, when she uses this term, her patients might think of severe tension. Then she uses the common term, high blood pressure. However, this term needs further clarification for patients from some foreign countries because high blood pressure can often be mistaken for someone who has an extensive volume of blood in the body.

Acronyms

There seems to be an endless number of acronyms. An acronym is a word that is composed of the first letters of other words. It is representative of more than one sequential word. Thus, acronyms are very efficient. Some of the well-known acronyms are IBM, which stands for International Business Machines; ASAP, which means "as soon as possible;" and C.O.D., which stands for "cash on delivery."

An acronym can represent more than one combination of words and can therefore become subject to misunderstandings. In an emergency room, a patient overheard the nurse talking to the physician, who referred to the patient as an S.O.B. As a result, the patient was quite upset but did not reveal his feelings. Shortly after his release from the hospital, he wrote a letter of complaint to the management of the hospital, emphasizing that referring to a patient as an S.O.B. is offensive and unprofessional.

After an investigation into the matter, the management promptly responded to this misunderstanding. They stated that S.O.B. is a common medical acronym that relates to patients who are "short of breath."

My Misunderstandings

The following two cases explain how my good intentions turned into misunderstandings. The first incident was from my high school years, and the second incident was caused by having different perceptions of protocols.

Following a Role Model Too Closely

Sometimes in our daily and common interactions with others, certain things happen with such an impact that we may never forget them. The following incident of misunderstanding is one of them.

In my early high school years, I had a biology teacher, Mr. D., who was my role model. I was always impressed by his manner, sophistication, attire, and knowledge of the field. Often, after a clear explanation of a topic, he used the expression, "Thus, it is now fully obvious."

I wanted to become like him, particularly after I finished my graduate education and entered into my professional life. I visualized Mr. D.'s behavior and comments in my mind. On occasion, when I was at home, I practiced to be another Mr. D. I gradually felt that I was becoming a copy of my biology teacher. Not only was I walking like him when entering the classroom, but I also knew exactly at what point in his lecture he was going to use the expression, "Thus, it is now fully obvious." As a result, we started to say the term together.

The gross misunderstanding on my part was that I thought that Mr. D. and I now had a few things in common, whereas he thought I had the bad intention of mocking his behavior.

One day, as usual, I entered the classroom, imitating his manner of walking, and sat in my seat. During his lecture and demonstration of the cells in the peel of an onion, as usual, he again relied on, "Thus, it is now fully obvious," which I said concurrently.

Noting that I had done that repeatedly throughout the semester, Mr. D., whose patience with my behavior had reached its end, stopped lecturing. With his loudest voice, he shouted at me, saying, "I am fed up with your mimicking behavior, and I want you immediately out of my class."

The problem did not end there, since in my naïve mind, I could not imagine that his anger was directed toward me. I thought we were friends because of our commonalities, and I thought his comment was toward the student sitting behind me. I turned back to that student and said, "Don't you get it! Mr. D. wants you out of the classroom. What are you waiting for?"

Again, he thought I was trying to disturb the class by being funny. While coming toward me, he shouted, "I am talking to you, and I mean you!" He went back to the podium, placed his books in his briefcase, and rushed out of the classroom, saying, "That's the end of it, as long as you come to this class."

The principal, who happened to be nearby, heard him. When he came to the classroom to find out what had happened, one of my classmates told him that Mr. D. had suddenly become frustrated with me, put his books in his briefcase, and left the school.

As we have seen, the misunderstanding was that I was admiring my teacher, but I failed to transmit the message the way it was intended, and ultimately it was interpreted as my being disrespectful. After the clarification by my parents and my formal apology, I was readmitted to class.

Diversity of Protocol

During my first few months at Colorado University, I was invited to a social event and was asked by a friend if I could give a ride to another attendee because she preferred not to drive. I gladly accepted the request. That evening, when we arrived at the event, I expected her to leave the automobile so I could lock the doors.

On the other hand, she expected that I would get out and open the door for her. Unaware of her expectations, I asked her to open the door and exit the automobile, so I could lock the doors.

Later, through a mutual friend, I was told that she found me to be a sociable person, but with a shortcoming in my social protocol because of my not opening the automobile door for her. Of course, I learned what to do the next time.

Shortly after this experience, I found myself in a similar situation. As soon as I stopped the car, I opened the door on my side, went around the car, and gracefully opened the door for my passenger. I was expecting some kind of recognition, such as "thank you." Quite to the contrary! It was in the midst of the feminist movement, and she happened to be one of the proponents of the movement.

She was truly offended by my opening the door for her. She declared something along the lines of, "Do you think I am not capable of opening the door, and I need your help?" I was unbearably confused because not opening the door for a woman was a problem, and opening the door for a woman was another problem.

A similar situation occurred when a young lady and I drove to an event. Arriving at our destination, I said to her, "Listen, with all due respect, do not ruin my evening, and please don't get upset, after all, it is only a door."

She was staring at me like I was out of my mind! I continued by saying, "If you want me to open the door for you, just tell me so. If you do not want me to open the door, simply say so. If you prefer to open the door for me for any reason, please feel free to do so."

She was quite confused by my concern about who should open the door. She politely said, "Why does opening the door seem to be an issue for you?"

I said, "Believe me, if you went through what I have been through, you would say the same thing." Later, I explained my experiences to her, and she could not stop laughing.

Intentional Misunderstanding

Interestingly, misunderstandings are more than seldom intentional. They are a way to create confusion for different reasons, as we will see. They can occur within an organization between a manager and employees or between an organization and customers. They can also happen on an interpersonal level.

Ambiguity of Department Policy

Robin was a software specialist in a large technology corporation. In one of the departmental meetings, the head of the department mentioned the importance of a dress code. Robin asked if wearing blue jeans was allowed. The department head replied, "Yes, only on an 'occasional' basis."

About two months later, both Robin and another employee were reported for violating the dress code set by the department head by wearing blue jeans. As a result, Robin and some other employees wanted a specific explanation of the word "occasional." The response they received was that all employees should "use their own judgment" as to the frequency of wearing blue jeans. Clearly, there was no reason to leave such a policy to personal judgment when they could have been specific about it.

Soon, the issue of creating such deliberate ambiguity came out in the open. The reason was that the human resources unit of the corporation was the only department with the authority to make organizational decisions on the dress code. With this understanding, on the one hand, the department head did not want to see his employees being so casual. On the other hand, he did not have the authority to formulate or enforce such a policy.

There are other motives for creating ambiguity or misunderstanding, some of which are reviewed below.

Playing Neutral

In one of the well-known drug manufacturing firms, there is constant friction between the technology department and the quality control department. The technology department is eager to come up with new products and send them through the production department to market them before competitors do. This relatively

71

fast-paced process may result in an approximate one-percent quality defect rate in the marketed products. The quality control department, on the other hand, insists on a zero defect rate.

When this matter came to the attention of the CEO of the corporation, he intended to maintain ambiguity. The CEO has extensive sales and marketing experience and favors fast-paced production. This way, not only will the drug company become a pioneer in providing a given product to the market, but it will also make the stockholders very happy. The other side of the matter is that anything greater than a zero percent defect rate is a risk with regard to the health of the patients and a serious threat to the reputation of the company.

Additionally, if the CEO insists on maintaining a zero defect rate, it would ultimately disenchant the technology and production departments. Should he be willing to compromise with a lower level of quality, it would disappoint the quality control department as well. Therefore, brushing off the matter and maintaining some sort of ambiguity was a selected alternative for the CEO.

Don't Have Any Appetite

In most Western countries, when acquaintances or extended families go to a restaurant, it is common that there will be separate checks for each party in the group. In some other countries, the check usually goes to the older person, unless otherwise specified to the server.

On one occasion, five individuals went to a restaurant. Among them was a clever man with a fatherly look and graying hair who knew that the check would probably come to him, something that he did not want to happen. Therefore, while in the presence of the waiter, who was ready to take the orders, in a casual and subtle way, the man declared, "I don't know why I have really no appetite at all."

This was a way to imply that he should not pick up the tab. One of the individuals at the table said, "We don't want you to be hungry. Why don't you have something light, at least!"

The man responded, "Well, since you insist, I will."

In the end, when the server brought the bill, he didn't know to whom to give it. The formation of this ambiguity by the clever man worked for him, and someone else had to pick up the tab.

Written Information

When reading about the benefits that you are entitled to with your health insurance coverage, did you find it hard to understand? A manager of the human resources department of an accounting firm shared the following with me. He pointed out that some health insurance companies intentionally write down the benefits that are provided by them in a rather confusing way. The purpose is for the insurance holder to be unaware of all the benefits. He also added that he has come across some insurance claim applications with intentional complications to discourage the submission of a claim. For example, requesting many dates of events that would be difficult to remember.

Final Notes

In this chapter, we reviewed the many faces of misunderstandings within and between various cultural settings. Some ambiguities were crafted and others were unintentional. We explained and demonstrated the simplicity of creating inadvertent misunderstandings with its wide range of outcomes. An understanding of the communication process and its dynamics is an effective approach to dealing with many communication breakdowns.

ENDNOTES

1. John H. Cushman Jr. "Avianca Pilots Blamed by U.S. In '90 L.I. Crash," The New York Times, May 1, 1991, P. B4., Ed Magnuson "Can Planes Just Run Out of Gas?," Times, February 12, 1990, p. 24; James T. McKenna, "CVR Shows Avianca Crew Knew Fuel Was Too Low," Aviation Week and & Space Technology, April 2, 1990. pp. 52-3.

2. "Air Travel: How Safe?," Time, April 11, 1977. pp.22-26; "KLM Pilot on Collision Reportedly Didn't Hear Controller's 'Stand By'," The New York Times, April 9, 1977. p.2.

3. "Minister De Transportes," Joint Report K.L.M.-P.A.A. 12.7. 1978, Colision Aeronves Boeing 747 PH-BUF DE K.L.M. Y Boeing 747 N 736 PA de Pan Am En Los Rodeos (Tenerife), EL 27 De Marzo De 1.977., 12.7.1978., PP. 59-60.

4. Ibid.

5. Matthew L. Wald, "The Colombians Attribute Cali Crash to Pilot Error," The New York Times, September 28, 1966. P. 12.

6. Ibid.

7. Gerald M. Golghaber, Organizational Communication, 3rd. ed. (Dubuque, IW: Wm. C. Brown, 1983), p.124.

8. Ibid.

9. John W. Newstrom and Keith Davis, Organizational Behavior: Human Behavior at Work, 9th ed. (New York: McGraw Hill, 1993), p.91.

RECOMMENDED READING

Andrew J. DuBrin. *Human Relations: A Job Oriented Approach.* Englewood Cliffs, NJ: Prentice Hall, 1992.

Deborah Tannen. *That's Not What I Meant!* New York: Ballantine Books, 1986.

Iris Varner and Linda Beamer. *Intercultural Communication in the Global Workplace.* Boston: McGraw Hill/Irvin, 2005.

James T. McKenna, *"CVR Shows Avianca Crew Knew Fuel Was Too Low,"* Aviation Week & Space Technology, April 2, 1990, pp. 52-53.

Joint Report, K.L.M.-P.A.A., *Collision Aeronaves Boeing 747 PH-BUF De K.L.M. Y Boeing 747, N 730*

PA de PAN AM En Los Rodeos (Tenerif), El 27 De Marzo De 1.977

Keith Davis. *Popular American Colloquialisms: Their Meaning and Origin.* Tempe, AZ: Keith Davis, 1991.

Stephen Manes, *"When Trust in Data' Is Misplaced,"* The New York Times, September 17, 1996, p. C9.

Richard Watkin, *"Mistakes That Doomed a Jet Are Crash's Biggest Mystery,"* The New York Times, January 1, 1990, p. 8.

CHAPTER FOUR

~

MANAGEMENT
AND
COMMUNICATION

In this chapter, the terms manager and leader will be used interchangeably, although there are fundamental differences between them.

1. A manager is more concerned with exercising authority over the day-to-day operations, while a leader inspires and motivates for productivity.

2. Managers are more task-oriented, while leaders show more concern for people reaching their goals.

3. Managers often mitigate risk by adhering to rules and policies, while leaders embrace risk-taking, challenges, and creativity.

Ambiguity in Managing

Oliver, the Director of Student Retention and Enrollment at a private higher education institution in Washington, D.C., attended the institution's semi-annual meeting, where the CEO was scheduled to recognize him and a few others for their achievements. After the ceremony, toward the end of the meeting, the CEO was responding to questions from attendees. Oliver asked whether he might be entitled to hire a few additional admissions officers for his department, considering the recent increase in student enrollment.

The CEO became irritated by the unexpected question. He made it clear that everyone works and is compensated accordingly. Therefore, there was no such thing as "entitlement" in this organization. To get his point across, the CEO demoted Oliver to his previous position, and a few months later, Oliver left the organization.

Since English was not Oliver's first language, he appeared to believe that 'entitle' was an elegant substitute for 'permission. The meaning we assign to a word can have an impact on our career and future.

Communication in organizations is becoming more complex, leaving more room for ambiguity. For example, in traditional organizations, purchasing personnel had to communicate with one superior to give reports or receive purchasing instructions. Nowadays, such a buyer typically also needs to communicate with the budgeting department to determine the allowed maximum purchasing price. Additionally, the buyer needs to communicate with the department responsible for the equipment purchase to obtain information about specifications and performance. The buyer also needs to consult with their immediate superior in the purchasing department.

The aim of this chapter is to discuss several concerns of communication that hamper overall organizational effectiveness within organizations. We begin with the employee interview process.

Joanne is a supervisory administrator in the human resources department of a mid-sized healthcare clinic in Maryland. One of her functions is conducting yearly performance reviews of the personnel. Joanne has the authority to increase an employee's salary up to five percent per year, depending on the level of displayed performance.

Linda is among the highest-performing nurses in the clinic. She also goes out of her way to help patients, physicians, and other nurses in the clinic.

This is the time of year when Linda's performance is evaluated by Joanne. In this year's appraisal, the overall quality of Linda's work is exemplary, with no shortcomings noted. As always, she has wonderful interpersonal skills with everyone, superior knowledge, and spends more time in the clinic than normally expected of nurses.

Given these considerations, Joanne gladly offered Linda the full allowable salary increase of five percent.

From Linda's perspective, this offer is not sufficient vis-à-vis her level of performance. She wants a raise of at least eight percent. Despite being in agreement with Linda's view, Joanne cannot offer Linda any more than a five-percent increase in her yearly salary.

Disenchanted, Linda decides to take her case to John, who is Joanne's immediate superior. It does not take too much effort to convince John to agree to a raise of eight percent.

The Possible outcomes of this occurrence could be as follows:

1. Ambiguity is created for Joanne. John, on several occasions, has emphasized the importance of following the rules and policies of the organization. Yet, he himself ignores them. John's instructions tend not to be taken seriously by Joanne.

2. Although Linda is happy because she received what she requested, she is rather confused and even suspicious of Joanne's sincerity. In the performance review, Joanne had acknowledged Linda's superior work, and yet she did not seem to care enough to give her an eight-percent raise in salary.

3. It was a lesson for others who witnessed Linda's actions: if you complain enough, you can get what you want in this department.

Situations like this are not uncommon. Incidents of ambiguities and misunderstandings often occur in many aspects of organizations that impact their performance.

Mission Statement and Practice

An organizational mission states the organization's philosophy and purpose, such as emphasizing its commitment to providing customers with world-class quality products. I have come across organizational mission statements that inadvertently convey an organizational vision by describing future goals, such as aspiring to become a global organization. The purpose of a mission statement is to inform customers about what the organization stands for and, based on the information, what the customers should expect of the organization. Additionally, the declaration of philosophy and the purpose tend to foster a spirit of unity and teamwork among the management and employees of the organization. A statement of the mission also provides useful information to other stakeholders, such as investors and business associations. The following are samples of mission statements:

Spotify

"To unlock the potential of human creativity by giving a million creative artists the opportunity to live off their art and billions of fans the opportunity to enjoy and be inspired by it."

Disney

"To entertain, inform, and inspire people around the globe through the power of unparalleled storytelling, reflecting the iconic brands, creative minds, and innovative technologies that make ours the world's premier entertainment company."

BBC

"To act in the public interest, serving all audiences through the provision of impartial, high-quality and distinctive output and services which inform, educate and entertain."

American Express

"To become essential to our customers by providing differentiated products and services to help them achieve their aspirations."

General Motors

"General Motors' corporate mission is to earn customers for life by building brands that inspire passion and loyalty through not only breakthrough technologies but also by serving and improving the communities in which we live and work around the world."

3 M Company

"Improving Lives through Innovation and Action - 3M. At 3M we seek to observe, understand, and solve. What we believe is simple: We are people committed to helping other people. Every day we help tackle problems, big and small, in pursuit of our vision to improve every life."

The Mission Statement for Nonprofit Organizations Goodwill

"To enhance the dignity and quality of life of individuals and families by strengthening communities, eliminating barriers to opportunity, and helping people in need reach their full potential through learning and the power of work."

ASPCA, The American Society for the Prevention of Cruelty to Animals

"To provide effective means for the prevention of cruelty to animals throughout the United States."

The Center for Disease Control

"CDC works 24/7 to protect America from health, safety, and security threats, both foreign and in the U.S. Whether diseases start at home or abroad, are chronic or acute, curable or preventable, human error or deliberate attack, CDC fights disease and supports communities and citizens to do the same."

These are statements of remarkable companies that take their mission seriously. On the other hand, there are many companies with appealing statements that exhibit little concern for people and their environment. Their statements are simply ceremonial. An organization may state that it cares about teamwork, but there is no spirit of teamwork and unity. An organization may state it cares about its employees while it has a high rate of turnover. Finally, an organization may point out the importance of customer satisfaction for its sustainability, yet the reality does not match the statement. As an example, I will relate my experience at a local dealership. Last year, I took my car to the dealership for its first oil change and general checkup. When I made the appointment, I was asked if I could wait for an hour instead of going home and coming back to pick up my car. I agreed to wait. While waiting, I saw the dealership's mission statement elegantly written and placed in a beautiful frame. The statement emphasized the dealership's commitment to friendly customer service and punctuality. However, during my visit, the staff was unfriendly, and there was an hour-long delay before my car was ready.

Employment: Interview and Evaluation

The job interview is a key step in the hiring process, assessing the alignment between the job description and job specifications.[1] This step is also an opportunity for the interviewee to learn more about the organization while deciding to work for it. Some of the conditions that impede effective interviews are as follows.

Halo Effect

This term can be defined as a snapshot of someone's appearance, behavior, verbal communication skills, or knowledge as a base for developing a generalization about that individual.

Experts in job interviews often stress the importance of a job seeker's appearance. A male with combed hair, a clean-shaven face, and a conservative suit and necktie would display a positive image of himself to the interviewer. He appears to be an intelligent and professional individual. This perception may or may not be correct. Additionally, when a job seeker successfully and accurately answers the first and second questions pertinent to the job content, the interviewer can form a positive perception of the job seeker's competence. Conversely, a job seeker who appears at an interview with sloppy clothes and fails to provide the correct answers at the beginning may minimize their chance for success.

Projection

An unconscious process in which an individual attributes their own thoughts, beliefs, or way of life to others. For example, someone who has a habit of exaggerating when describing an event to make it more exciting may assume that others have the same habit. In other words, when such an individual listens to an interesting event, he may feel that it has been inflated.

Projection can be unfair in many situations, including hiring practices. Mr. F., an interviewer for a furniture manufacturing company, is a rather introverted and unsociable individual. He attempts to display a sociable and friendly façade only when the situation requires it. Mr. F. interviews a job seeker who is well-mannered and friendly, but he may perceive that the job seeker's manner and friendliness are superficial, like his own. As a result, Mr. F. may offer the position to a less qualified individual.

Contrast in Perceptions

Perception refers to one's view of reality, such as someone or something that is subject to change. Suppose the chair of an academic department is interviewing several candidates for a full-time teaching position. Suppose also that the first few candidates are able to impress the chair with their teaching experience and other academic qualifications. The next candidate, Professor H., has his own set of qualifications, but they are not quite as impressive as the others. On a comparative basis, the chair may perceive him to be less qualified than he really is.

In an opposite scenario, if the chair has interviewed a few candidates who barely possess the minimum required qualifications, then Professor H.'s qualifications would look considerably better.

The chairperson may develop a less favorable perception of Professor H. in the first situation and a more favorable one in the second. Similar qualifications could be perceived differently by the same individual.

Groupthink

Generally speaking, conformity is important to a group's maintenance and decision-making process. However, an emphasis on conformity while overlooking the purpose of group formation leads to what is known as groupthink, which potentially results in unwanted consequences.[2]

Recently, one hospital on the East Coast announced several position openings for well-qualified psychiatrists. The hospital offered competitive salaries and a series of attractive benefits. Of the many applicants, only a few were selected for interviews based on their qualifications and credentials. Each candidate was interviewed by a panel of interviewers, and finally, a few psychiatrists were selected for the positions.

After the panel interviewed each candidate, the interviewers had a meeting to discuss their views on the candidate. One of the interviewers was apprehensive about hiring Mr. P., who was one of the candidates. The interviewer refrained from discussing his concern about Mr. P. during the meeting, and Mr. P. was eventually hired for the psychiatric section of the hospital. A few months later, it was found that almost all of this submitted credentials and documents were falsified. Subsequently, he was dismissed from the position. The question is, why did the interviewer, who was apprehensive about hiring Mr. P., not bring the matter into the open during the meeting for the selection process? It was because the interviewer happened to be the youngest and the least experienced member of the panel. He felt insecure about disagreeing with the other interviewers, who had predominantly positive impressions of Mr. P. This is a typical case of groupthink. Therefore, it is essential to create an environment that encourages all group members to speak openly, regardless of their level of experience or position.

Focusing on Results

All too often, the assessment of performance is based solely on the outcome, which by itself creates misunderstanding regarding employee performance. The way in which a job has been done must be taken into consideration for performance evaluation. The following experience illustrates this concept.

In most large furniture stores, it is typical that each sales associate takes a turn helping the incoming customers; therefore, each associate should have an equal chance to make a sale and earn the sale's commission. In this process, there are some sales associates who try to talk to more than one customer at a time without considering the other associates' turns to approach customers. Many of these sales associates also tend to be overly assertive with the customer in trying to make a sale. Therefore, these sales associates could affect the mood of other associates on the floor. Also, a customer may purchase an item but may never want to come back to that store, which ultimately would be a loss to the store.

Having that illustration in mind, we see that a salesperson may achieve the highest sales performance using this behavior, but at the cost of being unfair to other sales associates and driving away many customers. Performance appraisal should not only account for a given result but also for the employee's means of achieving that result.

Misleading Information

Providing misleading information emerges in many organizations, and can happen between managers and employees. The manager says, "You should have your promotion very soon," while knowing such a possibility is very minimal. The manager's misleading comment is intended to keep the worker on the job longer because of his high performance.

Many workers also come up with comments that are not straightforward. I know of an administrative assistant who used to have migraines frequently, especially every time she found herself in an overloaded work situation. As a result, the work was directed to others for completion. Later, because of her educational background and her know-how in a specific area, she was promoted to another position that she enjoyed. Since then, her migraines seemed to have disappeared.

Giving insincere comments also happens with or by people outside of an organization. Mr. B. was the owner of an educational institution with about three hundred employees. Occasionally, friends or acquaintances would go to him seeking a position. One of his acquaintances, Ms. J., contacted him for a position. For the purpose of saving face, Mr. B. assured her that he would send a strong recommendation to the pertinent department.

Mr. B. contacted the department head regarding Ms. J., but indicated that he did not want her to be part of the organization. Ms. J. did not know why she was not hired, despite the recommendation by the president of the organization. The point here is that Mr. B. was giving positive responses to Ms. J. to maintain a good relationship without the intention of helping her with employment.

In this section, I will refer to two areas of concern related to superiors and employees. First, I will discuss the deliberate formation of ambiguity and inconsistency of behavior as a seemingly effective approach to productivity. Second, I will discuss the inconsistency in providing feedback to employees.

Creative Ambiguity

Some years ago, I was engaged in consulting for an accounting firm. I noticed that one of the managerial practices of the firm was to hire graduate students from reputable universities for entry-level accounting positions. This way, the new entrants had the opportunity to gain first-hand experience while the accounting firm was able to pay them a lower salary than experienced accountants.

One of the departmental managers, Mr. D., was working with about twelve of these new accountants. He was more demanding of his employees than most managers in the firm. Mr. D. was sometimes quite sociable, friendly, and helpful, but other times, he chose to be quite the opposite. Because of the noticeable variation in his behavior, it was difficult to communicate with him.

One summer morning, I was in my temporary office when one of the new accountants wanted to speak with me in private. She hesitantly asked me if she had done something wrong. Surprised by her question, I replied, "No, nothing that I know of." On the verge of tears, she said that this morning she had seen Mr. D. in the hallway, waved at him, and said good morning. She saw no expression on his face as if she were not there. He then looked down while passing her. I told her that she should not take this personally, since he had probably had a bad day. Soon after this incident, another similar situation occurred with another new accountant.

In an informal gathering, my curiosity encouraged me to ask Mr. D. about his change of behavior in the workplace. He pointed out that sometimes creating a state of ambiguity motivates employees to be "on their toes." "If they cannot read my mind, then they prefer to do their best," he said.

Unsuccessfully, I voiced my view that ambiguity is worrisome to employees and decreases the productivity of their work. Also, as a matter of fairness, management should form a suitable working environment for employees. Gradually, through interaction with Mr. D., the new accountants came to recognize the motive for his behavior.

Personality Types in the Workplace

Individuals' personalities fall between two broad categories, personality A and personality B. Each category has its own distinct set of characteristics. For example, those with personality A tend to be in a rush, trying to perform more than one task concurrently. They are goal-oriented with an urgency to finish work before its deadline. They are competitive and prefer hard work over leisure. On the other hand, people with personality B are more laid back and less competitive. They appreciate relaxation.

An individual with a strong personality A working with a person with a personality B, could result in disagreements and misunderstandings. The following is a scenario of such a situation.

In the admission department of a large university, John was recently hired as the director. The new director had an assistant,

Joanne, who had been working in the same position for several years.

The director was not very efficient in his work vis-à-vis his highly demanding tasks. Additionally, the director was an obvious personality A and wanted to do even more than was required and meet all the deadlines beforehand. On the other hand, his assistant was very efficient with a laid-back approach.

Each day, the director gave Joanne several tasks to perform and kept wasting his time and Joanne's time by sending multiple e-mails for updates about the work progress.

John believed that Joanne was deliberately delaying the work so he would look "bad" in front of his superior, which was not the case. In the meantime, Joanne was thinking that John was trying to replace her by deliberately micromanaging her, which was not the case either. This case demonstrates how different personality types can lead to misunderstandings in the workplace.

Different Levels of Self-Confidence

It's important to have a healthy level of self-confidence when communicating with others. Self-confidence can range from being shy and ambivalent to being arrogant and egotistic. It's best to aim for a healthy level of self-confidence in the middle of that range.

During a casual social gathering, the discussion focused on the importance of effectively conveying a message. Someone shared an experiment that demonstrated the importance of self-confidence. At the beginning of the academic semester, the dean of the school of business introduced John Smith as an instructor of economics who had just earned his master's degree. The dean also mentioned that this class marked the beginning of John's teaching career. The instructor was dressed casually and delivered his lecture with a low level of self-confidence.

The next day, John was introduced as Dr. Smith in another economics class with 10 years of teaching experience and a Ph.D. from one of the best universities in the country. John was dressed professionally and delivered the same lecture as in the previous class, but this time with more authority and self-confidence in his field.

Despite the same lecture for both classes, the course evaluation results for the latter class were significantly higher than those for the first one.

Employee Motivation Overseas

An extensive study called the Hawthorne Experiments was conducted at the Western Electric Company near Chicago from 1924 to 1932. The objective of this experiment was to determine a solution for increasing the output of the company's workers. Initially, it was presumed that workers only work for money. However, the Hawthorne Experiments came up with a different conclusion. The study revealed that learning experience, teamwork, and less supervision were among the contributing factors toward a higher level of productivity. Soon after this illuminating discovery, many theories of human needs and motivation were developed to further investigate this issue. The best-known theory of needs and motivation is Maslow's, which I briefly referred to in the first chapter of this book. Maslow asserts that human needs fall into five sequential categories, which are:[3]

5. Self-Actualization

4. Esteem

3. Love

2. Safety

1. Physiological

From a managerial perspective, Maslow's hierarchy of needs theory can have the following interpretations. Physiological needs are money and salaries for the employees. Safety refers to job security and a protected work environment. Love denotes the feelings of belonging and being part of a given group in the organization. Esteem indicates the need to be recognized and appreciated for the good work done. Finally, the highest level is self-actualization, which is about creating an organizational culture in which the employees can do their best.

The invaluable benefit of Maslow's hierarchy of needs theory to management is that people come to an organization to work in order to satisfy a bundle of needs. It is up to the management to recognize these needs and to motivate employees accordingly.

The contents and the order of this theory are not always applicable to all cultures. In some cultures, for example, loyalty and status are notably more important than esteem needs. Not long ago, in one of my classes, I presented this theory for discussion.

One of my students stated that this theory should have been upside down. His explanation was that physiological needs, such as food and shelter, are more or less available, and therefore, should not be part of human concern. Instead, the main concern should be self-actualization.

To conclude, there have been two areas subject to misunderstandings. First, some managers may believe that people work only for money, which may not be the case. We have come across those who are not in need of financial compensation but who go to work for self-respect and self-worth. Second, as we have seen, such a theory, despite its popularity, cannot be generalized to all cultures.

Customer Satisfaction

It was midmorning one summer when I came home with my newly purchased desktop computer. I anxiously opened the package, read the owner's manual, and started its setup. On the panel of the computer, I saw an 800 number for technical support, available 24/7.

Seeing this made me feel comfortable about my purchase. Should I have any difficulty, someone would be there to help me out. During the process, I came up with a technical question. That morning, unsuccessfully, I tried a few times to speak with someone. Each time I called, I waited about fifteen minutes before hanging up the phone. Each time, there was a recording repeatedly apologizing for the inconvenience and assuring me that someone would be with me shortly. There was a discrepancy between what I saw on the panel of the computer for technical support and what I was experiencing.

Early that afternoon, I called again, and this time I was determined to wait as long as it would take to speak with someone about my technical question. I waited for about half an hour, listening to the same annoying repeated message. While waiting and holding the portable phone handset, I went to sleep in my rocking chair. It was over an hour later that I heard a voice saying, "Hello? Hello?" I woke up, and at first, I did not know who was calling me; I later realized it was the technician. I said, "Please don't hang up," then I asked my question. However, he could not really help me because he was new on the job, and no other technician was available to come to the phone. With considerable disappointment, the next day I returned the computer to the store, exchanging it for another brand. After this experience, I had no reason to believe that the company would be in business for long. About six months later, they went out of business.

Here is another scenario related to the issue of customer satisfaction that a bank teller shared at a gathering. She mentioned that in the branch where she works, there are not enough tellers to effectively help customers. As a result, the branch manager receives more than a few complaints about the long wait. This is how it happens. While waiting on a customer in the bank, the teller also needs to help the drive-through customers. Meanwhile, a supervisor comes to her with a question about an account. In the midst of all this, another customer calls, saying that she just received her statement, which shows a charge that cannot be accounted for. The teller explained that while the customer is waiting in line, she brings the matter to the head teller, who is also quite busy helping others. She tells the teller to get the customer's phone number for a later callback. For the customer who is upset and worried about the possibility of insufficient funds in the account, the word "later" is unacceptable. Understanding the customer's frustration, the teller goes to see the branch manager, but he is in a teleconference and cannot be interrupted. When she returns to the phone, the customer has already hung up. Soon after, the customer closed her account and wrote a letter of complaint to the corporate office.

It is puzzling that many corporations spend millions of dollars on their promotional activities, particularly advertising, to bring in new clients, while they pay almost no attention to keeping them.

Caring about Customers

In a graduate marketing course, a session was devoted to open discussions on the topic of customer satisfaction and loyalty. Names such as SAS, which is the world's largest privately owned software establishment, Nordstrom, American Express, LL Bean, Ritz Carlton, and Xerox were among many companies with excellent customer service reputations that were mentioned. But there were many others mentioned that provide substandard services to their customers. One of the students, who was working as a technician in a large communication company, shared the following experience.

Her job was to answer phones and speak to customers with technical questions. She asserted that, strangely enough, they were instructed not to pick up the phone promptly. The reason is to find out the average waiting threshold of their customers; in other words, how long it takes for a customer to become impatient and hang up the phone. This way the company can keep only the minimum number of technical representatives needed to keep their customers happy. The company's misunderstanding of this approach is that it may lead to short-term profitability by paying less in salaries, but in a competitive environment, it will threaten organizational growth and prosperity.

Thomas Jones and W. Earl Sasser, Jr. emphasized the importance of complete customer satisfaction. They reported that a comprehensive study conducted by Xerox Corporation revealed that

"Its totally satisfied customers were six times more likely to repurchase Xerox products over the next 18 months than its satisfied customers. The implications were profound: merely satisfying customers who have the freedom to make choices is not enough to keep them loyal."[4]

Why Are Companies Falling Short in Customer Satisfaction?

All of us have probably had a taste of receiving substandard service in one way or another. There could be an array of possible reasons for these experiences, such as employee work overload, lack of motivation, or lack of accountability. However, in this section, we can look at the lack of (adequate) commitment and loyalty on a reciprocal basis between employers and employees that can ultimately spill into customer dissatisfaction.

There have been numerous cases in which experienced employees were replaced by younger individuals simply to reduce salary costs. Many employees also leave their present jobs for even a slight salary increase elsewhere, overlooking years of built relationships.

With this condition of high employee turnover, an upper manager can anticipate leaving his present firm within the next few years. This upper manager, therefore, can select between one of the two following alternatives. The first is to purchase better equipment as needed, as well as provide various training programs, both technical and interpersonal, for employees. Of course, such an approach initially decreases organizational performance because employees will be spending time learning and training instead of being on the job to do their usual work. Moreover, there will be costs for training and purchasing advanced equipment. The end result is that for the first few years, the costs of operation will be higher with a lower production level. Such results may not be an addition to the credentials of that manager when he leaves that organization for another position. The second alternative would be to push sales and cut costs as much as possible. Therefore, the quality of both services and products are compromised, which ultimately affects customer satisfaction and organizational competitiveness.

Considering that a committed employee is the backbone of quality products and consumer satisfaction, I propose the following five interrelated steps: "the s Approach to Organizational Relationships." It is evident that the applicability and practicality of these approaches may vary significantly from one organization to another:

Connectivity

At this starting point, bringing about a better understanding of the organization's mission to its employees is essential. The management should communicate the organization's purpose and its

101

relationship with stakeholders, enabling employees to strive for a common goal.

Communication

Through a periodic, random sampling process, management can provide feedback to the employees. This could pave the way to open and sincere communication to uncover their fair and realistic expectations of the organizational management, such as job security, a variable pay plan, educational subsidies, or flexible benefit plans. The organizational expectations should be spelled out as well. Would they be paying more attention to quality products, teamwork, or coming forward with any pertinent problems or recommendations? As a result, the organization could formulate a realistic action plan that meets reciprocal expectations.

Coaching

The management of an organization should have the opportunity to seek assistance from outside consulting experts to assess the efficiency and effectiveness of its planning and implementation to receive insights as needed.

Cooperation

This phase denotes a give-and-take type of effort. The management commits itself to positive employee motivation while the employees are engaged in doing what they are supposed to do for the organization. The cooperation from one side tends to diminish with a lack of cooperation from the other side; therefore, continuous cooperation will set the stage for the next phase.

Commitment

Such a condition represents a sort of partnership between the two parties. Each side genuinely tries to do good work for the benefit of the other party striving for mutual benefit. The organization recognizes that its customer satisfaction and financial prosperity are embedded in employee satisfaction. Equally, the employee will be able to find a direct relationship between his commitment to his work and personal satisfaction.

Richard Florida and Jim Goodnight commented in the Harvard Business Review that there is a noticeable link between employee satisfaction and prosperity evident in SAS Institute, a software company located in North Carolina. SAS Institute is the most successful and the largest privately owned company of its kind in the world. A key focus of the company is its employees' satisfaction, and as a result, SAS is experiencing significant financial success.[5]

Management Effectiveness

As we are coming to the closing of this chapter, let me explore some of the aspects of managerial effectiveness. It is an oversimplification to assume that because one style of management is effective in one setting, then it will be effective in all situations. With this consideration, the following major components of effective management will be taken into account. (See Exhibit 4.1).

1) The manager's preferred style of management: Comfort Zone.

2) Determinant factors within organizations: Microenvironment.

3) Determinant factors outside of organizations: Macroenvironment.

Comfort Zone

The managerial style falls into three broad categories. First, laissez-faire is an approach by which managers allow employees to make decisions. They only call upon their manager as necessary. The second is the democratic approach, in which managerial decisions are made through collaboration with employees. The third is the autocratic approach, which emphasizes one-way communication. Managers make the decisions and announce them to the employees for implementation.

The preferred style of management is based on the way managers feel most comfortable. This may very well be because of the way they were treated as employees by their superiors. For example, one who has been working for an authoritarian manager could acquire the same style if that individual were to become a manager.

From the employee's perspective, there is a variation in desired managerial styles. "Employees in some cultures want their superiors to be ... decisive and authoritarian. Latin American employees, for example, may feel uncomfortable with a boss who delegates too much authority to them. In other cultures, such as those in the Scandinavian countries, employees want their managers to emphasize a participative, problem-solving approach."[6]

Microenvironment

Within an organization, four key determinants may influence managerial styles of leadership. The first has to do with the urgency to accomplish tasks. For example, when a fire department is notified of a "call" in a nearby building, there is no time for participative decision-making. The person in charge takes a course of action and announces it.

The second determinant is an environmental social structure that influences the way employees and their managers interact. In societies where formality is well-defined, it affects the organizational structures accordingly.

The third is the level of knowledge and expertise of employees. Employees who have acquired the desired know-how create a more suitable environment for participative decisions. Through this, managers are able to utilize their input and further improve both the morale of the employees and the quality of their products.

The fourth determinant concerns the importance of a quality product. In an organization that continually emphasizes quality improvement, participative management, which is employee inclusion in the decision-making process, seems to be most appropriate. Vertical communication should be intact. Managers instruct, guide, motivate, assign tasks, and provide feedback (downward communication). Employees ask questions, provide superiors with unfiltered reports for both progress and problems and are able to share ideas and suggestions with their manager (upward communication). Open, two-way communication is a major component of participative managerial style.

Macroenvironment

In addition to the comfort zone of managers and the determinants of the organizational environment, there is another area of concern: macroenvironment. The first concern is the attitude of society toward the pace of work. In many societies, hard work is a virtue. Someone once said that in Tokyo, it is uncommon for an individual to be walking in a residential area rather than being at work. However, in many other cultural settings, less work and more socialization and enjoyment of life are common trends.

Second, the issue of planning is a concern. In probably every textbook on management published in the United States, there is a chapter devoted to the process, importance, and range of planning.

However, not every society perceives planning to be highly crucial. This is because one may not be able to look into the future. In addition, the current era represents tremendous economic, technological, and political changes and unpredictability.

The third concern is regarding the degree of collaboration in the workplace. In some cultures, there is a minimal amount of teamwork. In many other cultural settings, such as those in most Asian countries, teamwork is reinforced because it creates synergy toward task accomplishments.

The observation of how people interact in social and business settings in a given society may provide us with some fair assessments of how people interact and communicate in respective organizations. The impact of the macroenvironment on corporate management is noteworthy. One of the multibillion-dollar European investment companies launched an extensive management training program for one of its overseas subsidiaries. The overall purpose of the training was to foster collaboration and participative decision-making in supervisory and mid-level management. However, the training programs were conducted without taking into account the external setting. The determinants of the macroenvironment in which the subsidiary was located were not in harmony with the intended managerial training programs. As a result, what had been learned in the training programs would soon evaporate.

Considering the reinforcement of the external setting, such training programs are not always a success. A higher level of effectiveness in training may be achieved by addressing these considerations. Managers, particularly those with international missions, should recognize the importance of assessing their managerial comfort zones as well as the determinants of the microenvironment and macroenvironment. Such assessment is helped by an open, impartial, and receptive mind. This is essential to selecting an appropriate managerial style.

EXHIBIT 4.1

DETERMINANTS OF MANAGERIAL EFFECTIVENESS

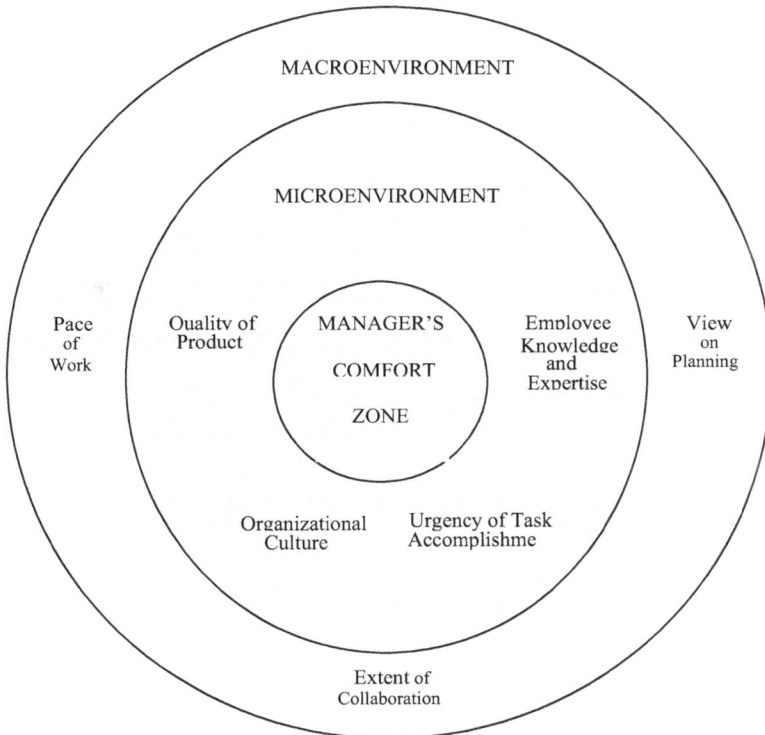

MACROENVIRONMENT

MICROENVIRONMENT

Pace of Work

Quality of Product

MANAGER'S

COMFORT

ZONE

Employee Knowledge and Expertise

View on Planning

Organizational Culture

Urgency of Task Accomplishme

Extent of Collaboration

Practicing Cultural Values in a Host Country

As stated in the Microenvironment section, the second determinant of the managerial comfort zone is what has been learned in the environmental social structure. It influences the way leaders and followers interact.

In societies where formality is well-defined, it affects the organizational structures accordingly. A renowned Dutch social psychologist, Dr. Greet Hofstede, in his comprehensive studies of national cultures, analyzes how managers and leaders exercise their level of authority. This study is about one of Hofstede's six dimensions of cultures, known as Power Distance.[7]

Power Distance

Initially, Geert Hofstede, in a theoretical framework, originated four dimensions of cultures:

1. Individualism-collectivism
2. Uncertainty avoidance
3. Power distance
4. Masculinity-femininity

Later, he introduced two additional cultural dimensions:

5. Long-Term Orientation vs. Short-Term Orientation
6. Indulgence vs. Restraint.[8]

The third dimension, power distance, focuses on high-power distance and low-power distance, which are related to potential misunderstandings in diverse organizational settings. In high-power distance cultures such as Venezuela, Indonesia, and India, decisions are made predominantly by the managers (leaders), and dialogue between them is formal. For example, an employee refers to the superior by the last name. In low-power distance environments, such as the Scandinavian countries, particularly in Sweden, participative decision-making is evident, and employees refer to their superior by their first name. The delegation of authority and decision-making is to the extent that less important decisions are made without the manager's approval.

It is oversimplified to assume that a specific level of power distance effective in the home country is universally applicable. A manager who subscribes to high power distance will commonly face many challenges working in a host country with low power distance. Such a manager is perceived as someone without much experience who hesitates to delegate authority and benefits from the input of experienced employees, which ultimately leads to discouragement and low productivity.

Managing with a low-power distance approach in an organizational environment that adopts authority, and formality can lead to confusion, employee morale, and motivation. The employees argue that their leader is paid more and well respected because of the earned knowledge and experience in the field. There is no reason why employees should undertake a part of the leader's responsibilities in the decision-making process. Furthermore, the leader does not manage the implementation of employees' decisions, raising the question of why they should participate in decision-making, a task that is reserved for management.

Final Notes

We have examined many pitfalls associated with hiring employees. We have also examined an understanding of the role of employees in customer satisfaction, which is essential in a competitive market. Another issue in complex organizations is in regard to the management itself. As described, each organization has its own norms and culture. Effective leadership is rooted in such understanding and the ability to adapt an approach conducive to overall organizational effectiveness.

ENDNOTES

1. A job description can be defined as a set of information that explains activities, duties, authorities, and responsibilities attached to the job, as well as working conditions and equipment. The job specification refers to the minimum qualification of the individual for the job, which includes both academic background and working experience.

2. Pamela A. Angel, Business Communication Design: Creativity, Strategies, and Solutions, 2nd ed. (New York: McGraw-Hill/Irwin, 2007), p. 293.

3. Abraham H. Maslow, "The Theory of Human Motivation," Psychological Review (July 1943): pp. 380-387.

4. Thomas O. Jones and W. Earl Sasser, Jr., "Why Satisfied Customers Defect," Harvard Business Review (November-December 1995): pp. 88-99, quoted in p. 91.

5. Richard Florida, and Jim Goodnight, "Managing for Creativity," Harvard Business Review (Jul-Aug 2005): pp.124-131.

6. John R. Schermerhorn, Jr., James G. Hunt, and Richard N Osborn, Managing Organizational Behavior, 4th ed. (New York: John Wiley & Sons, 1991), P. 87.

7. htpps://geerthofsted.com

8. Ibid.

RECOMMENDED READING

Donald G. Mosley, Paul H. Pietri, and Leon c. Megginson. Management: Leadership in Action. New York: HarperCollins College Publishers, 1996.

Gary Dressler. Human Resource Management. Upper Saddle River, NJ: Pearson Prentice Hall. 2005.

Gareth R. Jones and Jennifer M. George. Contemporary Management. New York: McGraw-Hill/Irwin, 2008.

Richard M. Hodgetts and Fred Luthans. International Management. New York: McGraw-Hill, 1997.

Wayn D. Hoyer and Deborah J. MacInnis. Consumer Behavior. Boston: Houghton Mifflin Company, 2007.

Houghton Mifflin Company, 2007.

CHAPTER FIVE

~

MARKETING AMBIGUITY

The field of marketing is not immune to the intentional and well-planned formation of ambiguity. In our discussion, a range of examples of promotional strategies and other marketing activities will be given, particularly from international perspectives. To proceed, let us briefly review the evolution of marketing in the United States, as it will provide a base for our analysis. (See Exhibit 5.1)

An Overview of Marketing Evolution in the United States

The history of marketing is closely related to the supply of and demand for goods and services, consisting of three broad evolutionary eras.

The Production Era

Toward the latter part of the 1850s, the gap between the supply of and the demand for goods and services was significant. The ability to produce was much smaller than the need and the ability to purchase. The proverb "necessity is the mother of invention" applies here because this gap led the way to the formation of assembly lines and mass production, as well as the invention of many items, such as the dishwasher, the elevator, the telephone, the light bulb, and the television. Therefore, the concentration was on production, so the ever-increasing demand was met.

The Sales Era

In the 1920s, there was a continuous growing trend of assembly lines and improved efficiency in the production process. As a result, there was more availability of goods and services, which lessened the dependency of buyers on a single supplier. Producers and suppliers recognized the importance of bringing a larger variety of colors, sizes, packaging, functionality, and styles as a means to attract customers.

Simply improving the quality of a product was not sufficient to create a positive edge against the competition. It was time for the sellers to learn about the techniques of selling strategies for successful marketing endeavors. Some of them are as follows:

- Do not ask customers if they want to buy an item. Assume that they want to buy it. So, give them a choice: ask them which color they are interested in. Green or blue?
- Try to talk about the price at the end of the presentation. Once you capture their interest, then give them the price.
- Through listening and observation, find out who is the ultimate decision maker. If, for example, a married couple is looking for bedroom furniture to buy, pay attention to the person who seems to be the decision maker.
- Do not ask for a signature; ask for an autograph. The word signature might scare most buyers.
- In some cases, act as if this is the last item with the color and size that the customer wants. How lucky!

The advancement of technology, assembly lines, and mass production took the availability of products to a new high. Consequently, in the 1950s, there was no notable gap between the supply of and the demand for goods and services. Rather, the abundance of products created many choices for the buyers. As a result, a gradual change from a "sellers' market" to a "buyers' market" began.

The Marketing Research Era

There has been a dramatic expansion of technology, modernization, and innovation in many fields such as transportation, energy, health, agriculture, and communication. In addition to this trend, beginning in the early 1970s, we have seen a monumental amount of product importation into the United States.

When you enter your neighborhood drugstore to buy shampoo, you will see so many choices that it may become difficult to choose one among them. For example, there are shampoos for newborn babies, for those with colored hair, and for those with dandruff. There are shampoos for thin, oily, dry, curly, or soft hair. There are organic shampoos and shampoos with a variety of scents. The list goes on.

In addition to the drastic increase in productivity and imported products, both durable and nondurable, there was another factor that diminished the vigor of selling techniques. Customers were continually becoming more informed about the products that they wanted to buy, thanks to the easy availability of data, such as the fair market value of a given used car. Marketers, therefore, had to rely on extensive marketing research and product development to find their target market and provide those customers with the exact goods and services they wanted to purchase.

Exhibit 5.1

A Conceptual Gap between the Supply of and the Demand for Goods and Services During the Evolution of Marketing in the United States:

ERAS OF MARKETING DEVELOPMENT

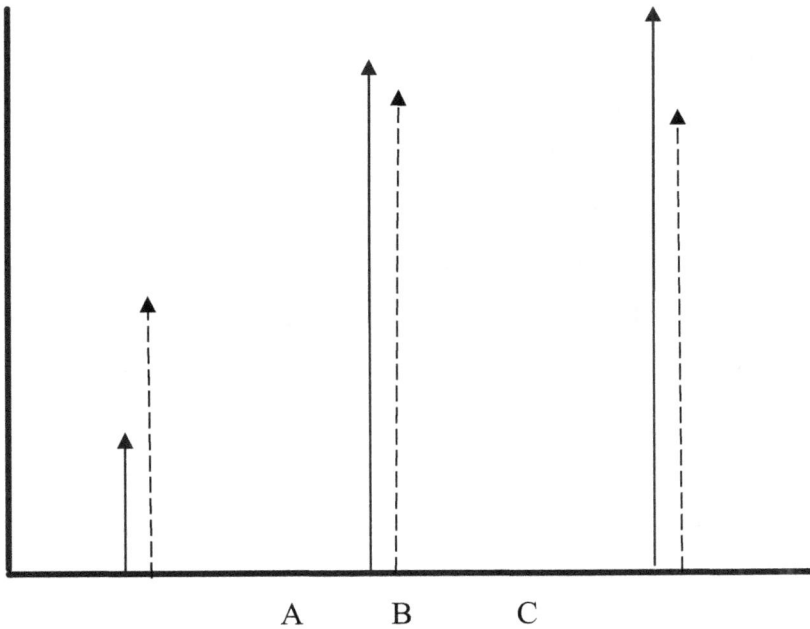

The Eras:

A → Production,

B → Sales

C → Research

Supply   Demand
  ↑   ↑
  | ¦
  | ¦
  | ¦
  | ¦

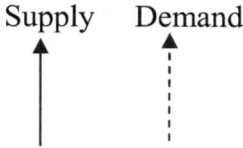

Nordstrom is one of the most successful upscale clothing department stores in the United States. The chain has an unflinching commitment to customer satisfaction. I have heard about a customer experience with the store. In the 1970s, a customer walked into a Nordstrom department store to return a pair of tires for a refund. Apparently, the location used to be a tire store, where the customer had purchased the tires. He simply wanted to return them to the same location where he bought them. The associate saw the price tag on the tires and accordingly refunded the customer for the tires.

International Strategies

There are four distinct strategic alternatives for becoming international. **Ethnocentrism** relies on domestic extension. Since certain goods or promotional activities are successful locally, they should work everywhere. Therefore, there are no reasons to make changes for markets across national borders, meaning a standardized approach. **Global orientation** companies take the standardized approach as well. The difference is that global companies conduct extensive marketing research in order to recognize and respond to the common needs and expectations of consumers on a worldwide basis. Multidomestic companies emphasize adaptation. They believe each market has its own unique characteristics that should be recognized, and they act accordingly. Finally, **Transnational** or **Geocentric** is a more complex approach. This takes advantage of worldwide efficiency through centralized decision-making for certain aspects of operations while delegating decentralized decisions to branches in different regions of the world for adaptation.

Do people prefer product similarity or differentiation? Not all authorities in the field of marketing share a similar view on this topic. Subsequently, these divergent views pose a challenging reality for multinational corporations (MNCs).

Theodore Levitt of Harvard University, in his well-known article "The Globalization of Markets," states that travel and communication are the two driving forces behind product standardization.[1] The benefit of standardization is a higher level of efficiency, allowing the company to become more competitive in the international market. Philip Kotler of Northwestern University agrees that there are situations that call for the standardization of the marketing mix. However, he directs our attention to many well-established products that failed in a global setting because of a lack of adaptation.[2]

In closing, in a general sense, I concur with Dr. Kotler. If people had preferred and moved toward standardization in our towns and streets, we would have seen cars of similar brands and colors, as well as similar optional equipment. We would have also seen similarities in women's dresses, and men would all be wearing about the same color of jacket. In the world of business, we are witnessing fierce competition at both the individual and corporate levels to become more successful and different.

Encountering the Unexpected

Not all marketers prioritize customer loyalty and satisfaction. Many choose various strategies to remain competitive. Most of us have encountered unexpected marketing techniques, which can lead to misleading perceptions about specific products or services. They could have been intentional or coincidental, pertinent to pricing or the quantity of products, or promotional strategies, a few of which will be examined.

No Matter What, I Am the Winner

While living in Colorado, one day, as usual, I opened my mailbox for incoming letters. On top of the other mail, I saw an envelope with bold letters stating that it was urgent, and I must open it immediately, which I did. There was good news! I was the winner of an expensive new automobile or an eight-carat genuine diamond. To claim my prize, I needed to drive to Brackenridge, Colorado, and participate in a sales presentation to buy land or a condominium.

It seemed too good to be true. In other words, I knew there had to be a catch, but I did not know what. Out of curiosity, my family and I drove to the designated location and participated in the sales seminar. There was a sales team that tried in many ways to close a sale, which created a very unpleasant experience. In the end, when we claimed our prize, we were told that we did not win the automobile but the diamond ring instead. But again, there was a catch, as I initially expected. Can you guess what it was? Was the diamond genuine? Yes. Was it of less total weight than specified? No. Was it of poor quality? Not necessarily. The fact was that the ring was composed of enormous particles of diamonds that were glued together. Apparently, these tiny pieces were gathered during the shaping and cutting process of the genuine diamonds. That was our prize! Something with no appeal and no value was immediately placed in a trash can.

Misleading Volume

There was an advertisement on television showing a man with a fit body walking in the woods while eating crunchy cereal. He was placing his thumb and forefinger in a full box of cereal, grabbing some, and putting it in his mouth. This advertisement stayed in my mind as I related health and nature to eating cereals. In another advertisement, there was a happy family at a breakfast table, having their cereal with milk. One morning, I arranged a table similar to the one I saw in the advertisement and enthusiastically headed to my neighborhood grocery store to buy a box of cereal. I could not find what I saw on television, but I bought another that looked appealing. While at the table, I opened the box and wanted to eat some of it before pouring it into a bowl. I reached into the box to grab some cereal, but to my surprise, I couldn't find any. I searched deeper into the box but still felt no cereal. Curiously, I looked inside and noticed that almost half of it was empty.

On my next visit to the store, I spoke with one of the employees about the box of cereal. He replied that almost all of them are that way, which I had a difficult time believing. Randomly, I purchased another box of cereal, mainly to satisfy my curiosity. The next day, I opened the box for my breakfast, and I realized that the employee was right—a significant portion of the box was again empty. On the cover, in very small type, there was an 800 number for customer relations. After a long wait, someone came on the line and asked many questions, such as my name, street address, and where I purchased the cereal. Needless to say, such data can be used as invaluable marketing data. I expressed my concern to the representative about the size of these boxes in relation to the volume of cereal inside. She commented that the boxes are actually full when they leave the plant, but they go through a settling process during transportation before customers purchase them. I then asked her if, as a customer, she would like buying a can of soup that was about 40 percent empty. I also proposed that they do the settling before the packages leave the plant to minimize misunderstanding. She replied that it was a very good point. She would share it with management, and someone would get back to me. To this date, no one from that cereal company has returned my call.

In many vending machines, you will see a pack of candies or pretzels that look full, as many of them are shown through a clear window. Once you put money in the machine to purchase them, you will soon find that about half of the bag is empty. This is because the contents of the bag are strategically placed. Notice that if you turned upside-down, it would look completely empty through that clear window.

Some years ago, some of my friends and I went to a restaurant. There, I saw large glasses of drinks brought to the tables, which were quite enticing. When the server was taking the orders, I asked for a soft drink with my dinner. A few minutes later, a large glassful of soda sat on our table. However, it was much less than it initially appeared. The reason was the unusual thickness of the glass.

Misleading Pricing

There was a program on television that showed how some department stores misleadingly claim that their products were on sale for 20 to 50 percent off storewide. The truth is, these stores set inflationary prices on their merchandise prior to sales. Afterward, customers are happy because they assume they are buying goods at discounted prices, which they are not. Another misleading approach in some department stores is when they claim that, for instance, a particular section of men's clothing is 25 percent off when in reality it is not, or it is discounted at only 15 percent off. Most customers rely on the credibility of the store and do not check their receipts.

There is another category of misleading pricing techniques. When I look at the automotive section of a local newspaper, I see many misleading messages. A dealership may say, "Huge savings, up to ten thousand dollars off, this weekend only." It seems like an attractive deal, but by saying "up to," the dealership could offer a discount of only a few hundred dollars.

An advertisement with large letters indicates that "For only three days, you will receive unbelievable savings." A new car that costs $25,000.00 is only $18,999.00. First, notice that this price is only one dollar short of $19,000.00, but more appealing. An asterisk next to the advertised price directs the readers to the bottom of the page. In very small letters that are hard to read or even to see, there is a

126

list of many exclusions that are normally least expected, like dealer's preparations and undercoating.

While writing this part of the book, I went to a supermarket to buy fruits and vegetables. As I was walking in the produce section, I noticed several piles of apples of different colors next to one another. I looked at the prices of the first few piles of apples, which were priced fairly per pound. I filled a bag with apples that were in the middle of other piles of apples. When I was paying the cashier for my purchases, I realized that the total price was more than I expected. Before driving away, I reviewed the receipt, and I noticed that the price paid for that bag of apples was quite high because the apples were sold per unit and not per pound. I returned to the store to verify the mistake, and I found that there were about seven kinds of apples. The price of each pile of apples was per pound, except for one pile. I was thinking as to why each kind of apple piled in one row sold per pound, with one exception. Was it a coincidence? What do you think?

Speaking of supermarkets and strategically placed items, often, items are placed on the shelves in a way that maximizes their exposure to sales. Among many, the following are three sample approaches:

First, necessary items such as bread, dairy products, meat, and vegetables are all placed as far as possible from one another. The idea is that to purchase these items, one must pass through all aisles in the store, which increases the chance that one will buy more or less important items. Second, more expensive products are placed closer to our eyes and reach. Items with less marginal profits are placed on the lower shelves. For children, because of their height, more expensive items are on the lower shelves to increase their exposure. Third, convenience products, such as chewing gum and newspapers, are placed close to the cashiers. While waiting, we are more prone to purchase these low-priced items.

In the following section, we will examine advertisements (a term that I use interchangeably with "commercials") and brand labeling in international settings that failed to provide intended messages.

Hidden Agenda

It was a few weeks ago when I visited a friend of mine, Fred, at his home during his recuperation from total hip surgery. During my visit, the telephone next to him started to ring, and a talking caller ID announced that his physiotherapist was on the line. Thinking that Fred did not want interruptions, I asked him to answer the phone at once, as it was an important call for him. He smiled and said, "At first, I was thinking the same way." He continued by saying, "They wanted to perform more physiotherapy than was recommended. At first, I said to myself that they are such caring people, but I found out that the more they visit me, the more they can charge the insurance company. I don't know if they are physiotherapists or telemarketers."

There was a time when full trust was given to most professionals because it was assumed that they wanted the best for us. It seems that this view is becoming a misunderstanding, as many of them think more of their own ends than of what is best for their clients. There have been, for example, many cases of unnecessary surgery done on patients, insurance agents who want to sell more insurance coverage than is needed, and representatives of private schools who call students with annoying frequency to get them to register.

Ambiguity in Product Promotion

This section concerns itself with four types of ambiguity in advertisements, as illustrated in Exhibit 5.2, below. They consist of:

- Verbal and Intentional
- Verbal and Unintentional
- Non-verbal and Intentional
- Non-verbal and Unintentional

More than expected, there is a wide range of unintentional misunderstandings in promotional efforts, notably in advertising. For instance, I have come across an advertisement that pictures a living room in which family and friends are gathered. It becomes difficult to understand the purpose of such an advertisement. Would it be the carpeting, the living room furniture, or the designer outfits that the picture is trying to promote? The advertisement fails to emphasize the intended product clearly. Some promotional experts, however, believe that these kinds of advertisements are well-thought-out and well-planned, and they are intentionally used to entice the viewers' curiosity.

The probability of creating a less effective or even counter-effective advertisement is considerably higher in international settings. The underlying reason for this is that promotional planners overlook cultural variations from one market to another. As stated in Marketing Week, "It is quite an art to tweak the content and presentation of advertising in different countries to produce a universally acceptable message."[3] Kitcatt Nohr, as an example, advertised in the United Kingdom, showing pet owners hugging their pets. This advertisement lost its effectiveness in Italy because it is not common there to hug pets.[4] Therefore, assuming cultural uniformity across nations creates misunderstandings that diminish promotional effectiveness.

Timotei Shampoo started selling its products in Taiwan, showing advertisements with a picture of a blonde woman. The Taiwanese women did not feel comfortable using the brand because they mainly had black hair. Later, the brand made the appropriate change to fit the market perception.[5]

It is also essential to be mindful of the differing meanings of words, brand names, and slogans across cultures. For example,

Chevrolet, a division of General Motors, expanded the sales of its Nova to some of the Spanish-speaking countries, including Mexico. In their initial market entry, they noticed people's reluctance to buy the Nova, which probably occurred because in Spanish, "No" means "no" and "va" means "go."

If an advertising campaign is successful in one market, it does not guarantee its success in another market, despite considerable cultural similarities and shared language. Electrolux launched a successful advertising campaign in England with the slogan, "Nothing Sucks Like an Electrolux." However, in the United States, the message was interpreted based on its colloquial meaning.[6]

Some years ago, I consulted for an American shoe manufacturer who wanted to explore the Western European markets for exports. The company specializes in men's shoes with thick soles. The initial plan was to disseminate catalogs and samples of its shoes to prospective intermediaries and major department stores. Although the company was successful in the American market, I advised more studies before implementing their plan. The reason was that a major portion of the American market prefers men's shoes with relatively thick soles that signify quality. However, Western European men favor thin soles on their shoes. Therefore, the manufacturer was looking into the possibility of adapting to that market by making shoes with thin soles or exploring other markets.

As noted, not all ambiguous advertisements are unintentional. Many advertisements are well planned and executed to be misleading and ambiguous. A billboard shows a young woman with full and shiny hair. Next to the woman is a bottle of shampoo. The objective is to develop an association between such attractive hair and this brand of shampoo, while the woman had beautiful hair to begin with.

Many advertisements claim that their product is the best. It is not clear that "being the best" signifies which characteristic of the product is best. Would it be its performance, durability, warranty, size, or style? Moreover, is it the best in comparison with other similar products in the market? The objective is to relate the term "the best" to their product.

Many advertisements intentionally create positive attributes about their companies or products, while they fall short of backing up their claims or statements. For example,

"Award-winning," but who gave the award?

"As seen on TV," but when and on which TV station?

"We guarantee our products." How?

"A study reveals that…" Which study?

"We beat the competition…" In terms of quality, quantity, or other characteristics?

Some advertisements claim that the offer is "time sensitive" and urge buyers to hurry and purchase their products before they are gone, as only a limited number of items are left. Why would a seller invest time and money in advertisements if they know that only a limited quantity of their products is available and that these items will sell out soon, regardless of their advertising efforts?

Exhibit 5.2

PROMOTION AND AMBIGUITY

Verbal/ Intentional	**Verbal/ Unintentional**
Nonverbal/ Intentional	**Nonverbal/ Unintentional**

Copyright © 2011 Bagher Fardanesh

Product Manufacturing and Corporate Ownership

Not too long ago, I was talking with a gentleman who was standing next to his Buick Century 2003. He was expressing pride in driving an American automobile. At that time, I noticed a label on the driver's door stating that the car was imported from Ontario, Canada.

The reality is that more than ever before, corporations manufacture their products across national borders, and the change in corporate ownership is occurring more frequently. Consequently, identifying the country in which a product is manufactured and the nation of origin of the corporation can be challenging. To this end, let us take a few moments to answer the following multiple-choice questions:

1. Godiva used to be owned by a (n) _____ company and now, it is owned by a (n)_____ company.

   a. American, Belgian

   b. Belgian, Saudi-Arabia

   c. American, Turkish

   d. Swiss, Belgian

2. Giant Foods' ultimate parent company is in _____.

   a. The United States

   b. The Netherlands

   c. Canada

   d. The United Kingdom

3. Greyhound Bus Line's ultimate parent company is in_____.

   a. The United Kingdom

   b. Japan

   c. The United States

   d. Luxembourg

4. Holiday Inn Express' ultimate parent company is located in _____.

   a. The United Kingdom

   b. Japan

   c. Canada

   d. The United States

5. Ben & Jerry is owned by which of the following companies?

_____.

    a. Unilever

    b. General Mills

    c. Kraft Food

    d. Nestlé

6. The first Subway restaurant opened overseas was in

_____.

    a. Cairo

    b. Buenos Aires

    c. Vienna

    d. Bahrain

7. Gerber baby food was acquired by a company in _____.

    a. Germany

    b. Austria

    c. Australia

    d. Switzerland

8. 7-Eleven stores' ultimate parent company is in_____.

    a. Norway

    b. Japan

    c. The United States

    d. Sweden

9. Anheuser-Bush is a(n) _____ company

    a. German

    b. Belgian

c. American

d. Japanese

10. Michelin is a(n) _____ company

    a. America

    b. Germany

    c. Italian

    d. None of the above

The answers to the above nine questions are:

1. c., 2.b., 3.a., 4.a., 5.a., 6.d., 7.d., 8.b., 9.b., 10. d

Commercials

Effective commercial campaigns are critically important to organizations; otherwise, ineffective promotions will lead to failures and disappointments. This section will discuss major components of successful commercials, mainly related to global settings.

Taking into Account Norms and Expectations of Viewers

Marketing messages must be in harmony with the norms and expectations of the target market. For example, in general, Japanese, compared to Europeans and North Americans, prefer to see a commercial that mostly generates feelings rather than facts.[7] So in Japan, advertisements about the performance and price of a product, particularly those that concern comparison with the competition, are not a common practice.[8] Therefore, even if a commercial is

137

successful in the United States, it may not secure the same results in Japan.

What makes the matter more complex is that music in an advertisement may evoke different feelings and sentiments from one cultural setting to another. A soft drink company advertised its product with hip-hop and rap music in a few industrialized countries. The campaign resulted in great success. The soft drink company decided to continue with the same approach in one of the emerging markets. Soon, it realized that those customers preferred native traditional music in the advertisements.

Regard for Legal Aspects of Commercials

Launching a commercial campaign in a new market necessitates careful inquiry into legal constraints.

As an illustration, in 1973, the Federal Trade Commission clarified that comparative advertising is not an unfair practice.[9] However, in many countries, including some in Western Europe, comparing one brand with another is prohibited.

Which products can or cannot be advertised is also an important consideration. J. Thomas Russell and W. Ronald Lane pointed out that "For example, fresh eggs may not be advertised in France, and cruise advertising is not allowed in Italy."[10]

Marketers should also be cognizant of nudity or messages with sexual connotations in their advertisements. The extent to which these approaches can be practiced varies significantly across countries.

Decision-Making Process

The topic of appropriate decision-making is critical to any organization's success. Almost any book on management and organizational behavior has a chapter devoted to this topic. As earlier stated, decision-making is divided into two broad areas: centralized and decentralized. Centralized is when decisions are made by the manager or a higher authority, whereas decentralized refers to employees participating in the decision process

Centralized decision-making has its advantages. It delivers more uniformity of delivered goods and services. It also provides a better way to monitor pertinent performances and take corrective actions as needed. Moreover, it is a device to minimize duplication of the work process.

On the other hand, decentralized decision-making delivers its advantages, among which the following can be stated. Decentralized decision-making involves entrusting those who are involved in the work process with the authority to make decisions. That could help boost employee morale and motivation. Also, as a rule of thumb, decisions made by several individuals instead of one or a few individuals deliver better results.

In the case of promotional strategies in international landscapes, decentralized decision-making has an underlying advantage. It is advisable to delegate the authority to make decisions to the local subsidiaries rather than decisions emanating from the headquarters. The reason is that decisions can be made and implemented more efficiently by those who are more familiar with the local market. It is a particularly invaluable approach when a quick response to the competition, such as in pricing, is needed.

Appropriate Translation

More and more, international corporations are relying on well-thought-out translations of slogans or messages to prevent distorted meanings.

There is also a growing number of organizations specializing in translation. Through both primary and secondary research, they focus on how the meaning of a given message is interpreted across different cultures.

Per Capita Income and Level of Literacy

There is a host of considerations in advertising campaigns. The credibility of a given channel of advertisement is one thing that should be taken into account. For example, sending coupons or notices of sales to individuals is known as direct marketing by the marketers, whereas it is mostly known by the receivers as junk mail and is placed in the trash can. At this point, we refer to two important matters related to the effectiveness of advertisements.

Per Capita Income

There have been frequent situations in which marketing decisions have failed to take into account the purchasing power of their target market and have subsequently caused unfavorable outcomes in their commercial campaign. In many countries, the average yearly income per individual is less than $2,000.00. In such markets, advertisements for large packages of specific products or advertisements for expensive items may lose effectiveness.

Concerning per capita income, it is important to note that, for example, country A might have a higher per capita income than country B, but country B could be a more suitable market because of its higher purchasing ability. Why? It is because of the favorable monetary exchange rates and the pricing structures of that market. Therefore, it is important to look into both per capita income and the purchasing power of that given market.

Literacy Rate

Another important element to consider is the literacy level of the target market. Advertising with written descriptions might only be suitable in markets with a high literacy rate. In environments in which there is a low rate of literacy, written advertisements lose their effectiveness and, hence, should be in visual forms, such as billboards or similar channels of advertisements.

Final Notes

Often, a major portion of marketing investment is allocated to promotional activities. Yet, it has always been a thorny task to measure and conclude the specific level of effectiveness of such activities. One thing is clear: promotional efforts are complicated, particularly with respect to international marketing. Considering a new market without ample knowledge of its socio-cultural and other environmental conditions is like walking in the dark in an unknown area. Therefore, a promotional campaign for a new market should be crafted with care to minimize the risk of unwanted consequences. In the next chapter, I will discuss issues, concepts, and potential misunderstandings in negotiations.

ENDNOTES

1. Theodore Levitt, "The Globalization of Market," Harvard Business Review, May-June 1983, pp. 92-102.

2. Philip Kotler. Marketing Management, Millennium ed. Upper Saddle River, NJ:

   Prentice Hall, 2000), P.367.

3. "Overseas Media: Becoming worldly-wise," Marketing Week, June 17, 2004, p. 43. http://proquest.umi.com

4. Ibid.

5. David Kilburn, "Crossing Border. (Advertising Foreign Brand Products in Asia)," Adweek, April 14, 1997, pp. 22, 24.

6. Michael R. Czinkota, and Ilkka A. Ronkainen, International Marketing, 6th ed. (Fort Worth: Harcourt, 2001), p. 65.

7. Kate Gillespie, Jean-Pierre Jeannet, and H. David Hennessy, Global Marketing: An Interactive Approach (Boston: Houghton Mifflin Company, 2004), p. 418.

8. Ibid.

9. J. Thomas Russell and W. Ronald Lane, Kleppner's Advertising Procedure, 12th ed. (Englewood Cliffs, NJ: Prentice Hall, 1993), p. 474 10.

10. Ibid., p. 656.

RECOMMENDED READING

Kenneth E. Clow and Donald Baack. Integrated Advertising, Promotion, and Marketing Communications. Upper Saddle River, NJ: Pearson Education, 2007.

Louis E. Boone and David L. Kurtz. Contemporary Marketing. Mason, OH: South-Western, 2006.

Michael J. Etzel, Bruce J. Walker, and William J. Stanton, Marketing. New York: McGraw Hill/Irwin, 2007.

Philip Kotler and Kevin Lane Keller. Marketing Management. Upper Saddle River, NJ: Pearson Education, 2006.

Philip R. Cateora and John L. Graham. International Marketing. New York: McGraw Hill/ Irwin, 2007.

Subhash C. Jain. International Marketing Management. Cincinnati: South-Western College Publishing, 1996.

Warren J. Keegan and Mark C. Green. Global Marketing. Upper Saddle River, NJ: Pearson Prentice Hall, 2005.

William Well, John Burnett, and Sandra Moriarty. Advertising: Principles and Practice. Upper Saddle River, NJ: Pearson Education, 2003.

CHAPTER SIX

~

GLOBAL NEGOTIATIONS, PROTOCOLS, AND MARKET ENTRY

Consider someone who is driving in a residential neighborhood and sees a garage sale. The driver stops the car and walks toward the many items for sale. While he is looking at different bargains, he notices an attractive antique lamp, which he finds quite appropriate for one of the rooms in his house. The price is higher than he wants to pay, so he begins to negotiate with the seller and succeeds in purchasing the lamp for a very attractive price.

Negotiations can take place in many situations, for instance, when a patient negotiates with a physician's assistant to set a convenient date and time for an appointment or when two parties become involved in a negotiation for the time of their meeting.

Negotiation also takes place between an employee and the human resources department of an organization over salaries and benefits. Or it can be seen when a young boy bargains with his parents for a later bedtime.

In this chapter, I will present two broad areas of misunderstanding. One is the view that all negotiations are based on the notion of a zero-sum game, meaning that for someone to gain, someone else has to lose. The other source of misunderstanding in negotiation is pertinent to cross-cultural settings. Too often, business negotiators assume that because a given approach produced a successful result in their home country, it will be effective in host countries as well. In this chapter, I will also provide a number of case studies to deepen our understanding of the nature and dynamics of negotiations. Finally, I will open a section to show the many dos and don'ts of negotiations in cross-cultural landscapes.

Divergent Approach to Negotiation

There are two major approaches to negotiation: distributive and integrative. Each of them has its own strategies and expected outcomes that we shall review.

A Distributive Transaction occurs when one side or each side of a deal tries to gain as much as possible at the bargaining table with no or minimal concern for the other party. Such an approach often prevents long-term relationships and impedes future negotiations.

An East Coast Oriental rug and antique merchant shared the following with me to describe his strategy to purchase various items for next to nothing. He related that recently, an individual walked into his store carrying a rug of about 5 x 8 feet on his shoulder and was anxious to sell it. Although the merchant needed an area rug like that, he told him differently, "I am not interested in buying a rug with such colors and patterns. But to help you out, I can make you an offer," which he did. The man gave the offer some thought and reluctantly accepted it. While the seller was waiting for the check, the merchant looked at the rug again and said, "Oh, I didn't notice a hole in the rug and some imperfection in the pattern."

The merchant explained to me that the hole could have been fixed easily, and those imperfections were expected with handmade rugs. It is one way to differentiate between handmade and machine-made rugs. The merchant further stated that he knew the condition of the carpet at the very beginning when he first glanced at it, but pretended he did not as a way to lower the sales price even further. He said to the seller, "I cannot buy it for the price that I quoted you, considering these flaws that I did not notice earlier." Finally, the desperate seller agreed on a lower price, and the deal was completed. Soon after, the merchant sold it for a hefty profit.

The same merchant also shared the following. He occasionally receives telephone calls from those who want to exchange their old area rugs for new ones. Often, these old carpets are rare antiques. He told me, "I received a similar call only a few days ago from an elderly man. As per his request, I went to his home because he had a few antique rugs that he wanted to get rid of in exchange for new wall-to-wall carpeting, and I agreed to help him. He did not seem to be aware that for a fraction of the value of one of his antique rugs, he would be able to get wall-to-wall carpeting for his home."

Integrative Transaction is based on reciprocal consideration in negotiation as well as open communication among all parties. The main ingredient is fairness, which leads to satisfaction and long-term relationships among the involved parties.

One of the largest accounting firms in the Washington, D.C. area was, for several years, undertaking the tax preparation for a well-known entertainment company with many branches nationwide. The fees for the tax preparation were about $300,000.00. Each year, the accounting firm added about 5 percent to its fees to offset the inflation rate and to account for the expansion of the entertainment company.

For tax preparation in 2015, the top management executives of both the accounting firm and the entertainment company held a meeting. The purpose of the meeting was for the entertainment company executives to explain that, for the first time in eight years, they had had a bad financial year. Not only did their income not increase, but it was lower than initially forecasted. Therefore, they requested not to pay the usual 5 percent increase in tax preparation fees; additionally, the entertainment company wanted to pay a rate comparable to the fee they had paid two years ago. Their rationale was that the company needed to save money and cut costs as much as reasonably possible to create a base for future growth.

After a relatively short meeting between both sides in the negotiations, the accounting firm agreed to make an exception by going along with the request of its client.

Luckily, the entertainment company was able to return to its usual growth path in 2006, and subsequently, the accounting firm received its 5 percent increase plus an additional surcharge as compensation for the previous year.

The following occurrence, which I witnessed, describes how one can create a winning situation for both sides. It was only a few weeks ago that I walked into a chain car rental store to rent a vehicle. I noticed a customer ahead of me saying to a representative that he was not happy with the car he had rented the day before because the air conditioning was not working properly. He added that, as a result, it would be difficult for him and his family to keep the car until the next day, when they were scheduled to drop the car off at BWI airport.

The representative, John, could have responded in the following ways:

- He could have said that there was not much that could be done because the air conditioning was working properly at the time of rental, and it was now the customer's responsibility.
- He could have told the customer to fill up the gas tank, bring the car back, and then give him a similar car.
- He could have charged the customer for the consumed gas and given him a similar car on the spot.

However, John took a different approach in responding to the customer, which went like this:

John: "I am sorry for the inconvenience, and for that, I am going to give you our most luxurious automobile instead of another mid-sized car."

Customer: "Really?"

John: "Yes, sir!"

Customer: "You are not going to charge me more for the exchanged car?"

John: "No, we are not going to charge you any more than you were going to pay."

Customer: "How about the gas tank that is half full? Do you want me to fill up the car and bring it back?"

John: "That is not necessary. We will take care of it for you."

I saw a big smile of satisfaction on the customer's face.

After John helped that customer, he gave me a ride home because I had returned my rental. Having known John for about two years, I felt comfortable asking him this question on the way: What was the reason for his overly gracious gesture to that customer? He commented that there is nothing better than having happy customers in such a competitive business, especially when it does not cost you a penny. I asked him for a further explanation. John responded that luxury cars are expected to be much more expensive to rent, and because of that, there is much less demand for them. He added that that particular car had been in their lot for a few days, and as a result, they were losing money each day. John added that such cars, however, have more demand when they are at the airport. "Knowing that we did not have anybody to take that car back to the airport, my offer to that customer made us both happy, and what's better than that?"

The following describes the condition of multidimensional winning. Some years ago, I was in Colorado, where I became acquainted with a merchant of men's clothing. On one occasion, he shared an intriguing experience with me about the creativity of an independent wholesaler.

At one time, the wholesaler contacted the merchant, wanting to sell several large boxes containing designer shirts and accessories for men. The merchant expressed his interest in buying the merchandise, but said he could not afford it. He had many small shirts that he could not sell. On the one hand, he did not have adequate space to place more shirts; on the other hand, he did not want to spend more on something risky to sell.

The wholesaler noticed that all the shirts the merchant could not sell were in a small size, and the medium, large, and extra large sizes were already sold.

Relying on his problem-solving ability and creativity, the wholesaler proposed that he would be willing to buy all the leftover shirts if the merchant bought the boxes containing the designer shirts and accessories. The fact was that the wholesaler knew an international trader who was looking for small–sized shirts to export to one of the Asian countries where, on average, men are smaller in height than American men.

The negotiation resulted in satisfaction and profit-making for the international trader, the wholesaler, and the merchant.

No Room for Negotiation

In this section, you will notice two cases of negotiation. One of them is a case of understanding between the two parties that resulted in a done deal. The latter is a case of an unsuccessful negotiation as a result of a misunderstanding.

The Purchase of an Antique Painting

Mrs. M., who was from a wealthy family, had been looking for several months for a special type of antique painting for her living room. One day, when she was visiting a series of antique stores, she, surprisingly, came across exactly what she was looking for.

Mrs. M. contacted her uncle, who was a well-known and well-respected expert in antique items, including paintings. She wanted his opinion about the quality and originality of the painting, and she wanted to know what a fair price for it would be.

Through an arrangement, Mrs. M. asked her uncle, Mr. Z., and the owner of the antique shop to meet at her house. The owner of the store, Mr. N., was going to bring the painting with him to show to both Mrs. M. and her uncle, Mr. Z.

On the designated afternoon, Mr. N. arrived with two men who were carrying the painting. After the usual greetings, Mrs. M. enthusiastically said to her uncle, "This is the painting I was telling you about. What do you think?"

Mr. Z. was such an expert in antique paintings that he did not even care to examine the painting closely. All he said to Mrs. M. was, "Do you have your checkbook with you?" She said, "Yes, here it is."

Mr. Z quietly told her the amount to write the check for, and she quickly agreed. Mr. Z. asked the store owner to come forward to receive the check for the purchase of the painting. Mr. N. saw the check and politely commented that the amount was much less than he expected and that it would not even cover his cost.

Implying that there was no room for negotiation and that it was a done deal, Mr. Z. intentionally said, "Have a good day; have a good day," implying that it was time for them to leave, which they did. Mr. N. thanked Mrs. M. and her uncle and left with his two employees, who had carried the painting to the house.

Note that the seller did not set the price, but Mr. Z. did. He was confident that the seller not only covered his costs but also made a fair profit. Knowing about Mr. Z.'s expertise and negotiation skills, the seller was aware that any attempt to bargain would have been a waste of time and would probably risk the sale of the painting altogether.

Bargaining in a Department Store

In many societies around the world, almost everything for sale is subject to negotiation. Negotiation is not only a way to determine a mutually acceptable price between the seller and the buyer, but it is also a means of socialization and a way to create customer loyalty.

A young man who came to the United States to study at a university went to a department store to buy a few things for himself and his newly rented apartment. While walking in the men's shoe department, he noticed a pair of shoes that he was interested in. He found a salesperson, and their exchange went like this.

Customer: "Do you have a pair of shoes like this, size half-past nine?"

The salesperson smiled and asked: "Do you mean nine-and-a-half?"

Customer: "Sorry, yes, that is what I mean."

Salesperson: "Yes, we do."

The customer tried them on and asked for the price.

Salesperson: "They are $129.00."

Customer: "That's too much money for a pair of shoes! How about if I give you $30.00 for this pair?"

Salesperson: "Sir, our prices are fixed; we cannot give discounts."

Customer: "You are a hard negotiator. Ok, I'll give you $50.00 for them."

Salesperson: "Our prices are fixed."

Customer: "This is my last offer, $75.00. I cannot go any higher than that."

Salesperson: "Sir, our prices are fixed; we are not allowed to give any discount."

Finally, the young man, who was not accustomed to buying something without negotiation and receiving some type of discount, had no choice but to pay the full price or simply not purchase the shoes.

He gave some thought to it and reluctantly agreed to pay the full price for the shoes.

The salesperson added the 6 percent sales tax and asked the customer to pay $136.74.

The customer, who was not familiar with sales tax, became puzzled by the new price. He asked, "Why can you not lower the price, but for one reason or another, you can raise the price? That is not right; you are trying to take advantage of me for liking the shoes by asking for more."

The young man was quite disenchanted because of the unsuccessful negotiation. He walked away without buying the shoes.

Negotiation is a strategically oriented art, and it should be handled with care. Otherwise, it could lead to conflict and misunderstanding, particularly when entering into a different cultural setting. This section will address many of these conditions.

Intercultural Negotiations

There are two different approaches in negotiations relevant to multicultural settings, as shown in Exhibit 6.1. Many business negotiations are destined to fail because some corporate negotiators are more concerned with time efficiency, while other negotiators emphasize the effectiveness of the outcomes. A team of negotiators relying on efficiency wants to begin negotiations soon after the meeting has started. In reaching a successful negotiation, gradual trust and friendship will emerge in the future.

A different approach is commonly embedded in establishing both trust and a sound interpersonal relationship among parties early in a negotiation. It is believed that negotiation without establishing a trusting relationship is like constructing a building with a shallow foundation, and is therefore more prone to breakdown.

M. Katherine Glover asserted that "Many nationalities value the personal relationship more than most Americans do in business. In these countries, long-term relationships based on trust are necessary for conducting business. Many U.S. firms make the mistake of rushing into business discussions...."[1] Many negotiators in Scandinavian countries and Canada prefer the efficiency of the process. However, most transactions in Egypt, Mexico, Japan, China, and the United Arab Emirates are based on effectiveness. Regarding the importance of interpersonal relationships in China for negotiation, Dave Archer notes that "The better your relationship, the better chance you have of negotiating a viable agreement that benefits both parties."[2]

When one party exhibits more concern about time efficiency and the other party focuses on effectiveness, this in itself leads to what I call "tempo differentiation" of the process, which potentially leads to transaction breakdown. One party may perceive that their counter-negotiators just want to "get down to business" and make a deal. The other party may perceive the situation differently, thinking that their counter-negotiators are not really serious or, for one reason or another, want to delay the deal.

Exhibit 6.1

NEGOTIATION PROCESS

People Focused

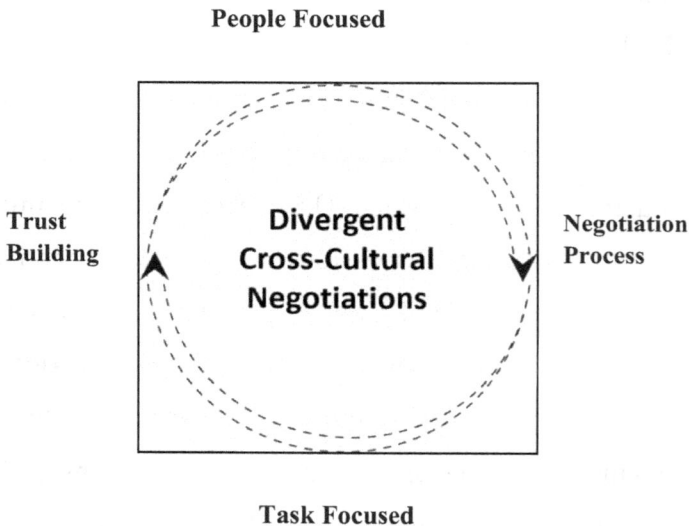

Task Focused

Copyright © 2011 Bagher Fardanesh

Connectivity in Negotiation

There are three approaches to negotiation in terms of connectivity and involvement.

First, there are some negotiators who pay full attention to what is being said by the other party. They also want to make sure that they are exhibiting their attention by refraining from doing anything but listening. Also, they occasionally rephrase what has been conveyed. This approach, on a reciprocal basis, can lead to successful outcomes.

Second, there are some negotiators who pay full attention to what is being communicated by the other negotiator, but meanwhile, they might be doing something else, such as looking at some papers or files. Periodically, they might say, "Go on, I am listening to you." This approach is grounds for misunderstanding because one party in the negotiation is listening to the other one but exhibiting behavior that sends a different message.

Third, there are some negotiators who pretend to be listening carefully, although their thoughts are elsewhere. Often, a negotiator who is not paying attention to both verbal and non-verbal messages, such as the tone of voice or facial expressions of the other party, is thinking of a response instead. One can imagine the outcomes of such a negotiation, in which each party, in lieu of being concerned with the comments and non-verbal cues of the counterpart, is only thinking of a comment in response.

Diverse Protocols and Beyond

In a business transaction, the two parties gather with good intentions geared toward successful results. However, a behavior or protocol that is common in one culture may be improper in another, interfering with effective negotiation. In this section, I will evaluate a number of these conditions.

The Art of Handshakes

There is much more to a handshake than what may appear. There are variations of handshakes in regard to their firmness, duration, and frequency. In the Middle East, for instance, handshakes are normally given with minimal firmness, but they occur quite frequently and with a short grip. In France and some other European countries, handshakes are relatively less frequent than in the Middle East. They are firm with a short grip. In the United States, handshakes are the least frequent, but they are quite firm and have a longer duration.

Lack of knowledge regarding the variation of handshakes from one country to another is a cause of misinterpretation. For instance, a warm handshake by one party may be taken as a lack of interest by another party.

Preparation of Documents and Their Submission for Signature

The content of any contract needs to be crystal clear before being brought to the table for signatures to prevent any potential embarrassment or legal complications. The format of the contract is also significantly important.

For example, some negotiators want to place their signature immediately after the content of the contract comes to an end, without leaving any blank space. This is to prevent the possibility of the other party in negotiation from adding more to the content of the contract in blank spaces above the signatures.

Another matter of importance is whether to exchange documents with the left or right hand. In some cultures, the left hand is for personal hygiene and should not be used for handling papers.

Often, communication concerning transactions or negotiations is via e-mail. In some countries, a delay in response is quite typical and should not necessarily be interpreted as a lack of interest.

Using the First or the Last Name?

In the United States, using first names is quite frequent among colleagues and co-workers. Americans commonly prefer to use someone's first name after the first or a few meetings. It is perceived as a gesture of closeness and friendship. On the other hand, the Japanese, , and French adhere to the use of the last name for a much longer period of time as a matter of protocol in formal organizations.

A few years ago, an American entertainment company was in the process of entering into a joint venture agreement with a Japanese firm. The American company invited a team from the Japanese firm to come from Tokyo to San Francisco for further negotiations. For the event, the first names of the attendees were written on identification tags.

Upon the return of the Japanese team to their corporate headquarters, a letter was sent to the head of the American company. Aside from their appreciation of the hospitality they received, they expressed their disenchantment over the use of their first names.

Dates on Documents and Letters

Another source of confusion is that in one country, such as Switzerland, when writing dates, it is customary to first write the day, then the month, and then the year. In another country, namely, the United States, it is customary to write the month, then the day, and then the year. Such a difference can create a lot of misunderstandings in terms of dates for meetings or contract signing.

Variations in the Customs and Protocols

Knowledge of the customs and protocols of the people with whom we are interacting is important for minimizing misinterpretations. Below is a sample of these variations.

- When making a point, Italians move their hands more frequently than the Japanese.
- In Saudi Arabia, it is rude to cross one's legs in a way that shows the bottoms of the shoes; in some other countries, crossing legs is a condition of informality.

- It is important to be on time in Germany and in Switzerland, whereas being about half an hour late in most South American countries is acceptable.

- In Iran, the bottom layer of the cooked rice, which is crisp and crunchy, is served to the guests as the best part of the rice, whereas in Pakistan, the top layer of the cooked rice is considered the best part.

- French negotiators welcome negotiations over lunch, whereas Americans prefer to talk about business after lunch. Also, having lunch takes less time in the United States than in France or other parts of Europe.

- Beer is served at room temperature in most parts of Europe, including Belgium, England, and Austria, whereas it is mostly served chilled in the United States.

- Americans often have a salad before their dinner, whereas the Swiss and most other Europeans have it served with their main course.

- In the United States, bouquets are made with an even number of flowers, often a dozen, but in Scandinavian countries, they are arranged with odd numbers.

- In China, unlike most other countries, sneezing should not be noticed by others.

Dynamics of Successful Negotiation

A long-time friend of mine, Saeid, provided an invaluable recommendation as part of the negotiation strategy. Last week, over a cup of coffee, I asked how he negotiated with multinational companies for favorable results. Saeid responded that he used to plan for a negotiation session. After many years of experience, he said during negotiations, his mind is constantly working in search of new strategies for that moment. More specifically, his strategy is highly adaptive.

Another important aspect of a successful negotiation is being aware of your BATNA before you start negotiating. It stands for Best Alternative to a Negotiated Agreement, a concept developed by Roger Fisher and William Ury.[3] Understanding your BATNA will help you determine whether the deal being negotiated is what you hoped it would be. If not, will you have another advantageous alternative available? An example of BATNA is: Suppose you are ready to buy a new car from one of the nearby dealerships. If the negotiation with the dealership is not successful, what would be your options? Will you buy a different brand from another nearby dealer or go to another city to find the car you initially wanted to buy?

Fisher and Ury also originated the term ZOPA, a Zone of Possible Agreement.[4] Let's assume the scenario shown in Exhibit 6.2. Randi has a used car that he wants to sell for $20,000, but he is willing to accept an offer of at least $15,000. Alicia has seen the car and is interested in buying it. She is willing to pay $14,000 up to a maximum of $17000 for the car. Fortunately, her highest offer falls within the price range that Randi is willing to accept.

Exhibit 6.2

Alicia
$14,000.

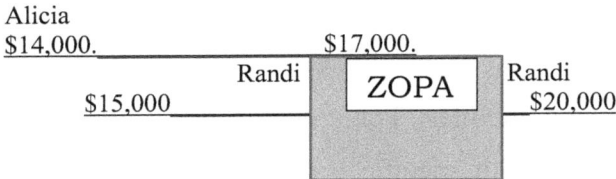

Negotiation

In a different type of negotiation, both the buyer and seller can become overly enthusiastic, leading to a scenario where the seller wishes to be paid less, while the buyer desires to pay more.

In a negotiation, each party seeks a favorable outcome based on its self-interest. For instance, in a car negotiation, the buyer aims to pay a lower price while the seller seeks to sell the car for a higher price. However, it is unusual for a situation to arise where the seller wants a lower sales price, and the buyer wants to pay more.

Imagine a situation where the seller wants to sell an item for a lower price, but the buyer insists on paying more. Jordan had a beautiful antique handmade rug that his parents gave him. After a few years, he decided to sell or give it away as he planned to move into a smaller apartment. Mia, a collector of antique rugs, offered Jordan a high selling price for the rug, which amazed Jordan. He thought the price Mia offered was more than fair, while Mia felt that she should have offered him more for the rug. This is a case where the seller is asking for less and the buyer insists on paying more.

From a macro perspective, there are situations where buyers are willing to pay more than what sellers are asking. There are many buyers ready to pay above the manufacturer's suggested retail price (MSRP) for certain automobiles. For example, there was high demand for certain cars with specific options, such as powerful engines. In the 1970s, buyers were particularly eager to pay more for models like the Pontiac Firebird Trans Am, Chevrolet Corvette, and Ford Mustang Mach 1, to name a few.

Similarly, in the housing market, certain areas such as San Jose, Miami, Austin, and Boulder experience such high demand that buyers often pay prices that exceed the original listings.

A Case of an Indecent Negotiation

Younes, a successful international businessman, shared an incident with me that is worth mentioning. He had a commercial property that he no longer needed and wanted to sell. Younes hired Alex to handle the bureaucratic process, prepare the property for sale, and find serious buyers. Through telephone conversations, Alex provided weekly progress reports to Younes.

After about eight months, Alex called Younes with the good news that the property was now ready for sale. He also said that he had successfully found three partners who were ready to purchase the property at the negotiated price and the conditions he asked for. However, Younes needed to travel overseas within one week to complete the deal. Otherwise, the potential buyers would purchase another property. Alex assured Younes that the cashier's check was ready, and upon signing the selling agreement, he would receive the check.

Enthusiastically, Younes canceled all of his appointments and purchased a round-trip ticket overseas. The day after his arrival, he attended a meeting with the three partners, their two lawyers, and Alex. After a few minutes of customary business protocols, about a dozen legal documents were given to Younes, awaiting his signature.

Younes noticed, with disappointment, that there was no cashier's check for him to have after he signed the documents. He hesitantly asked Alex and the others for the check. Alex, on behalf of the others in that meeting, mentioned that he first needed to release the property to the partners, and by the next morning, the check would be ready for Younes to pick up.

Despite the intimidating situation, Younes was smart to refuse to sign any documents and left the meeting. Soon, it became obvious to Younes that the man he had hired, Alex, and others in that meeting had created this charade to deceive him and take ownership of the business property without paying for it. In short, this was a case of double misunderstanding. First, Younes trusted Alex to protect his interests, but that did not happen. Second, the buyers acted as though they could fool Younes into giving away his property for free.

Five Guidelines for a Winning Negotiation

Five guidelines pave the road for a winning negotiation.

1. Once you make a statement, stop, and wait for the other party to respond.
2. Don't show too much excitement to close the deal.
3. In addition to knowing your BATNA, learn about the BATNA of the other party when possible.
4. Invite the other party to your office for negotiation. It puts you in a better position. Otherwise, choose a location such as a coffee shop to negotiate.
5. Some negotiation strategists recommend waiting for a few seconds to respond, which signals your reply has been well thought out.

Five Common Tactics, Game Play in Negotiation

Many negotiators rely on at least one of the following tactics for favorable negotiated outcomes. I will provide examples of car-buying experiences for the following tactics.

1. **Bogey** is when, for example, the buyer of a car pretends that, with the money the seller asked for, he can get a better deal at another dealer down the street.

2. **Nibbling** tactic often happens toward or at the closing when the buyer asks for a few more concessions, such as a floor mat for winter or an extended warranty.

3. **Intimidation** is when the salesperson and the sales manager engage in bullying the prospective buyer by exhibiting frustration, such as saying you wasted our time for nothing...

4. **Empathy** is a tactic that is more common in some other countries than in the United States. It's when the buyer asks for the seller's compassion to accept a deeper discount. An example of empathy is when the buyer says the car he wants to purchase is for his son, who needs it for transportation to college.

5. **Snowballing** is when the seller talks about the sophisticated technological advancement of the car and uses unfamiliar terms to confuse and overwhelm the buyer.

I Experienced a Snowball Tactic

Snowballing isn't restricted to negotiations because it's used to divert the other party from the main concern. I had health insurance coverage from one of the biggest insurance companies that consistently refused to pay their share of claims as they should have.

After being unable to resolve the issue on my own, I reached out to a manager in the claims department. He informed me that if I had Medicare Plan B, they would cover my claims. However, if I did not have Medicare Plan B, the company would assume that I did, but in either case, they would only partially pay my claims, deducting the co-pay.

I suggested to him, "What if you don't pay a premium and just 'assume' I did, is your insurance company still liable for paying my insurance claim? Would this be acceptable?" The manager adeptly responded with a fast pace and unclear comments in order not to respond to my concern. Luckily, with the help of another channel, I was able to resolve the issue.

Misunderstanding in Global Market Entry

Doing business in other countries can be both challenging and rewarding. A common conception is that because one type of market entry is successful in one country for a given product, it will have the same outcome in other countries. In most cases, such concepts are misleading because of differences in socio-cultural, economic, demographic, technological, geographical, political, and legal, as well as competitive conditions across markets.

There are many forms of market entry, such as licensing and franchising, turnkey projects, contract manufacturing, management contracting, and foreign direct investment (FDI). FDI can be in the form of joint-venture agreements or wholly owned subsidiaries. In this section, I will identify and comment on various pitfalls in the latter type of FDI because, often, wholly owned subsidiaries carry both a higher risk and profit than other types of market entry.

Perception of Foreign Products

In some cultures, people are attracted to foreign products because they see them as exotic or, at least, different. On the other hand, in some other cultures, the notion of ethnocentrism or cultural superiority persists. In such cultures, negotiations and the distribution of foreign products become exceedingly cumbersome.

Political Stability

The issues of confiscation and expropriation must not be overlooked. Both mean governmental takeover. Confiscation is a transfer of ownership without compensation, whereas expropriation is the transfer of ownership with some sort of compensation. When there is a history of political instability in a country, FDI becomes a very risky business. The marketer should consider other types of entry, such as exports to that country, to minimize the risk of loss of assets.

Ethical and Legal Aspects of Business Practice

This is indeed a challenging matter that causes considerable misunderstandings among people of different cultures. In many societies, bribery, for example, is unethical and even illegal. In some other places, it is a common practice. One explanation for this is the inadequacy of salaries of government officials and corporate employees in some parts of the world. In these instances, bribery and similar behaviors are means of supplemental income.

Although bribery has its own specific meaning, it is a generic term for similar behaviors. Below you will find the terms, definitions, and a relevant example for each of these behaviors.

Bribery

This occurs when one party requests that a corporate agent or a bureaucrat engage in illegal or unethical behavior in favor of that party in exchange for monetary rewards. A contractor may pay a member of a selection committee to vote in favor of the contractor to win the bid for a given project.

Cateora, Gilly, and Graham have defined the following unethical behaviors.[5]

Subornation

This happens when an individual, for personal gain, asks a responsible agent to overlook his illegal and unethical behavior in exchange for money. An example is when an individual is carrying some sort of illegal goods when entering a country. At the customs checkpoint, the individual offers a payment to the customs agent to ignore the items found in the baggage.

Extortion

This occurs when something of value rightfully belongs to an individual, but the responsible agent or bureaucrat who is in charge of delivering the item asks for a financial favor beforehand. Suppose you purchased an automobile in country X to be shipped to country Y. Later, during the process of paperwork for the delivery of your automobile, you notice that several agents ask for money to complete the process.

Lubrication

This can be defined as giving a negligible sum of money to a lower-level employee or bureaucrat to expedite a given process. For example, in some countries, people have to wait in line to cash a check. Someone who does not want to wait can offer an employee of the bank a tip to cash the check in just a few minutes.

Marketing Research

To minimize the risk of ownership or control over the operations of a subsidiary, one must conduct a feasibility study, which can be done through secondary and primary research.

Secondary research is relatively efficient and much less costly than primary research. Secondary research is comprised of reading governmental and other publications regarding the feasibility of entering a given market. Such exploration includes finding the level of demand for a given product, the level of competition, and the condition of a particular economic infrastructure.

It should not be overlooked that too often the collected data is either outdated or inaccurate, something more evident in developing countries. In some cases, a given government may deliberately publish inaccurate data to signify more favorable conditions for various reasons, namely, to attract foreign investments. Should the secondary research offer a favorable outlook, the marketer should consider the inclusion of primary research.

Primary research can be conducted through face-to-face interviews, telephone surveys, or reliable survey questionnaires targeting a specific market. Although the primary research approach generates more updated and more accurate data than secondary research, it has its own share of potential misunderstandings.

- Face-to-face data gathering can deviate from accuracy because of perceptual differences. For example, "a lot of snowfall" may not mean the same thing in Boulder, Colorado, as it does in Key West, Florida.

- Surveys via telephone in one culture may seem conventional, but in another culture, they may be considered obscene phone calls. Therefore, the receiver of the phone call may not respond or may deliberately provide inaccurate information.

- Written questionnaires can be troublesome because in many societies, most people cannot write or read their native language. Additionally, many questions can be considered too personal or even offensive. Therefore, respondents may not want to answer these questions, or at least not with accuracy.

The following exercises are provided as related to international business negotiations.

1. During business negotiations, crossing legs in _____ is considered inappropriate.

   a. Thailand
   b. Japan
   c. Bangkok
   d. All of the above

2. During business negotiations, eating food is common in _____ .

   a. United Kingdom
   b. United States
   c. France
   d. Switzerland

3. In _____, it is least common to exchange documents with the left hand.

   a. India

   b. South Korea

   c. Sri Lanka

   d. China

4. In business negotiations, eye contact is least often in _____ .

   a. The United States

   b. Germany

   c. Canada

   d. Mexico

5. After a brief talk, getting down to negotiation is most common in _____ and least common in _____ .

   a. Belgium, India

   b. Kuwait. Pakistan

   c. United States, Australia

   d. Austria, The Netherlands

6. Negotiations often take place over a drink in _____ .

   a. Malaysia

   b. Indonesia

   c. Australia

   d. India

7. Bargaining is common in _____

a. Sweden

b. Norway

c. China

d. The United States

8. Modesty is most respected in _____

a. Iceland

b. Spain

c. Norway

d. China

9. The business negotiation process is slower in _____

a. El Salvador

b. Norway

c. Canada

d. Romania

10. Individuals with older age are more appreciated for business negotiation in _____

a. Hong Kong

b. Bulgaria

c. Argentina

d. Sweden

Answers: 1.d., 2.c., 3.c., 4.d., 5.a., 6.c., 7.c., 8. d, 9. a, 10, a

Final Notes

Knowledge of the negotiation process involving a party of another culture and business protocols is significantly important when entering a new market. Knowledge of the advantages and disadvantages of each type of market entry is equally important. Also, learning about the external environment is another critical dimension of going forward on the path to success. In addition to what I have already presented , many other conditions need to be scrutinized, such as the practices of imposing protective tariffs, quotas, subsidies, and embargoes as major barriers to international trade. Also, when entering a new market, it is important to learn about the rates of inflation, labor laws, salaries, and similar pertinent matters, especially per capita income and its distribution pattern for that market.

ENDNOTES

1. M. Katherine Glover, "Do's & Taboos: Cultural Aspects of International Business," *Business America*, August 13, 1990, p. 3.

2. Dave Archer, "Doing Business in China," *The Journal of Commerce,* October 30, 2006, p. 64.

3. Fisher, R., Ury, W., and Patton, B. Getting to Yes: Negotiating Agreement Without Giving In, 2nd ed. (New York: Penguin, 1991).

4. Ibid.

5. Philip R. Cateora, Mary C. Gilly, and John I. Graham, *International Marketing,* 14th. Ed. McGraw-Hill, 2009.

RECOMMENDED READING

Charles Hill. *Global Business Today*. New York: McGraw Hill/Irwin, 2008.

Paul R. Krugman and Maurice Obstfeld. *International Economics*: *Theory & Policy*. Boston: Pearson Addison Wesley, 2009.

Scot Ober. *Contemporary Business Communication*. Boston: Houghton Mifflin Company, 2001.

Sondra Thiederman, *Profiting in America's Multicultural Marketplace: How to Do Business Across Cultural Lines*. Lanham, MD: Lexington Books, 1992.

Ricky W. Griffin and Michael W. Pustay. *International Business: A Managerial Perspective*. Upper Saddle River, NJ: Pearson Prentice Hall, 2005.

Terri Morrison, Wayne A. Conaway, and George A. Borden. *How to Do Business in Sixty Countries: Kiss, Bow, or Shake Hands*. Holbrook, MA: 1994.

Roy J. Lewicki, David M. Saunders, and Bruce Barry. *Essential of Negotiation*. New York: McGraw-Hill, 2007.

CHAPTER SEVEN

~

CONDITIONS
AND
COMMUNICATION

To enhance our understanding of the nature and types of misunderstandings, I will present a series of related cases. First, I will describe instances where I misunderstood others. Second, I will explain the concepts of success, effective leadership, cultural norms in conflict resolution, and the varying emphasis on teamwork versus competition in different cultural settings. Third, I will discuss the complexities of communication in international environments. Fourth, I will illustrate how a single word or phrase can carry different meanings, leading to misunderstandings. Finally, I will outline several guidelines for minimizing misunderstandings among people from diverse cultural backgrounds, some of which will have implications for successful communication within specific cultures.

Luckily, It Did Not Happen

I have already discussed a range of cases of misunderstanding, including those that have occurred in managerial activities, in business settings, and in marketing decisions. In this section, I present two cases of misunderstanding that were close to causing unpleasant results but, luckily, did not. This is to demonstrate the ease with which one can fall onto the path of misunderstanding.

Where Is My Pen?

A few years ago, I was taking a KLM flight from Schiphol Airport in Amsterdam to Dulles Airport in Washington, D.C. I was sitting next to the window. On my right, there was an empty seat that separated me from a middle-aged and professional-looking man. We were served lunch, and shortly after, with my black Mont Blanc pen, I started to make a list of the things I needed to do in the next few days. While writing, I felt drowsy and ended up taking a short nap. When I opened my eyes, I noticed my pen was missing; I had it in my hand before taking a nap. Unsuccessfully, I looked everywhere around my seat, on the floor, around my feet, and in my pockets, but I could not find it.

While thinking about where my pen might be, I noticed that the man on my right was using my pen. I did not know how to react or what to say to him. In this predicament, several possible alternatives passed through my mind. Should I ask him to give me back my pen, or should I complain to a flight attendant? Complain about what— tell the attendant that he has my pen without my permission? If he denies it, then how could I prove that it is my pen? Or, should I wait until we arrive at the airport and then speak with an airline representative?

While thinking about these alternatives, I started to have a very brief conversation with him, which was similar to this:

"Is this a Mont Blanc?" I asked.

"Yes, it is," he replied.

While looking at the pen, I asked him, "How long are you going to use it?" He did not know how to respond to my odd question, as he probably thought I was trying to begin a conversation with him.

"Well, probably as long as I need it," he responded.

By then, I knew my questions were futile and that I might make the matter worse by continuing to question him. A few minutes later, I saw that he had finished writing and had placed the pen in his jacket pocket. Seeing this did not help the situation.

Upon arrival at the airport, passengers began to pick up their belongings to leave the plane. I waited while others left the plane because I wanted to speak with a flight attendant or a representative concerning my experience. While waiting, I bent down to pick up my briefcase from under my seat. Most unexpectedly, I saw my pen, which was "hiding" behind my briefcase. Apparently, while I was taking a nap, the pen fell from my hand.

Hesitantly, I rushed to leave the plane to find the man so I could apologize to him and explain the situation, but could not find him.

Too Close to Break a Relationship

Mr. P. was the general manager of an automotive dealership that I had known for over 15 years. I always had pleasant experiences negotiating with him, to the extent that I recommended him to my close friends. About six months ago, I went to the dealership to purchase a car. I found that Mr. P. was no longer working there, but that he was with a nearby dealership. I went to the other dealership, and there he was. However, Mr. P. was not the general manager; he was the director of finance. He kindly introduced me to the general manager and the sales manager of the dealership. Through their help and collaborative negotiation, I was able to find a car at an attractive price.

I then had to go to Mr. P to take care of the paperwork. The purchase was without financing through the dealership. Among the many papers that I had to fill out, there were a brief loan application, one for the credit check, and one for the proof of insurance coverage for the new purchase. Content with my purchase and confident in

Mr. P.'s honesty, I was not concerned about signing the papers before me.

A couple of days after my purchase, I began to file the paperwork relating to my purchase, during which, ironically, I noticed that I had applied for a $4,900.00 loan. As a result, I drove to the dealership for clarification. When I showed the paper to Mr. P., he commented that the loan was meant for another customer and apologized for the confusion. Finally, the problem was resolved, and the loan application was destroyed. This incident led me to become more cognizant of each of the papers I signed at the dealership. In this process, I could not understand why I had given the dealership permission to check my credit history and provided them with proof of insurance coverage for the automobile, because I was not applying for a loan through them.

Three mistakes! Those were many mistakes for one purchase, so I was quite uneasy about the whole thing. I wanted to find out about their motive for asking me to sign those irrelevant documents. With all of the paperwork with me, I drove to the dealership to complain to the general manager concerning my experience.

While I was driving, my cell phone rang. The caller was a sales manager from another dealership who said that he had just located the car I was looking for. I informed him that I had already purchased one. In the meantime, while I had him on the line, I told him about my bizarre experience regarding the dealership's request for a credit check and proof of insurance coverage when I had not applied for a loan. His response was that there is a new law that requires dealerships to check each buyer's credit and requires buyers to provide proof of insurance coverage, regardless of whether or not they are requesting a loan. I was very appreciative of his explanation.

I turned around and drove back home. While driving, I was thinking about my misunderstanding and how close I had come to finding myself in a regretful and embarrassing situation.

Self-Misunderstanding

When we think of misunderstanding, generally it is about communication with someone, a condition, or an event. Misunderstanding can also be about ourselves or the potential that we possess. The following describes one of the most memorable events of my academic years.

About 15 years ago, I was teaching a basic management course at a four-year college. Occasionally, I had students whose tuition was paid by a not-for-profit organization. In such cases, I was asked to fill out a short report concerning a student's academic progress. The progress had to meet a minimum satisfactory level for tuition reimbursement.

In one of my classes, I had a student who was noticeably shy and withdrawn. Not so surprisingly, he earned grades below the satisfactory level. One day after class, when everyone had already left, he hesitantly brought his report card to me to fill out. I paused and said, "I hope you see the situation I am in. I cannot write that you are in good academic standing in my class while you are not. If I write about your low academic performance, then you will be faced with financial troubles."

As if he had an answer ready, he replied, "Just write down that I am not as smart as most other students. And, in fact, my counselor thinks the same way about me...." I interrupted him by asking him several irrelevant questions, such as the name of his favorite elementary teacher. He successfully answered all of them.

Puzzled by my questions, he politely asked me the relevance of my questions to his report card.

I replied "A lot! I see a contradiction here. If you were not so smart, then how could you remember the answers to these questions that I just asked you?"

The smile on his face and the glow in his eyes were unforgettable. He then came to recognize that he had underestimated his ability to learn and comprehend. I will never forget that this student earned one of the highest scores on the final exam.

Organizations and Cultural Diversity

Organizations are formed by individuals working coordinately and systematically toward a common organizational goal. There are many aspects of organizations that are subject to misunderstandings because of their variations across cultures. Below, I discuss the meaning of success from one organizational setting to another, effective leadership, different approaches to managing conflicts, and views on teamwork.

Meaning of Success

In some cultures, success is measured by a person's level of income, whereas in other cultures, success might equate with working for a multinational and globally known company. In some other cultural settings, longevity and affiliation with an organization indicate success because they indicate one's determination and stability. Yet, in other settings, having more responsibility, being promoted, or having a sophisticated title signifies success.

Therefore, it becomes obvious that a given managerial approach for motivating employees that would be effective in one culture may become ineffective in another.

Leadership

Leadership styles fall into three broad categories: laissez-faire, democratic, and autocratic. Tannenbaum and Schmidt, in their Continuum of Leadership, provide more details on leadership, which are as follows:[1]

1. **Abdicate**, when the manager allows employees to make the decision and announce it.

2. **Delegate**, when the manager allows employees to make decisions but sets the parameters.

3. **Engage**, when employees give ideas as a part of the manager's decision-making.

4. **Consult**, when the manager makes the decision, but consults employees before implementing it.

5. **Share**, when the manager makes the decision, but allows employees to ask questions about the decision.

6. **Convince**, when the manager makes the decision, but gives explanations for the decision.

7. **Tell**, when the manager makes the decision and announces it.

In some societies, managers are respected because they make decisions based on their knowledge and experience in such a way that affects employees and organizations. To maintain their respect, they must make decisions on their own and announce them. Therefore, soliciting input from employees signifies their lack of ability to make decisions independently. From another perspective, some employees argue that managers do not undertake part of their work, so they wonder why they should be involved in a manager's job, which is to make decisions and announce them. On the other hand, in some societies, employees strive for delegation of authority and participative decision-making. This style of management is a major source of employee motivation.

Conflict Resolution

Depending on the cultural setting, there are distinct approaches in organizations dealing with interpersonal conflicts. For instance, in some organizations, the common practice is to bring conflicts into the open, either on a face-to-face basis with the presence and involvement of the manager or in a departmental meeting. People share and discuss their differences and seek a resolution, mostly without developing hard feelings toward each other. In some other cultures, active conflict resolution through openly discussing a matter results in losing face, regardless of the outcome. In other words, initiating an open discussion may intensify the existing conflict.

Therefore, it becomes clear that a manager of an organization who is accustomed to a given approach for resolving conflicts should be aware that such an approach may be counterproductive in a different setting.

Teamwork and Productivity

Depending on a given cultural setting, the notion and practice of teamwork can vary. The rationale for promoting teamwork is that it creates a sense of unity and develops synergy in efforts toward task accomplishment. In some other settings, competition is emphasized. It is viewed as an indication of self-reliance and independence. Also, any prize or recognition will be given to the person who was actually the most productive. Therefore, competition is viewed as a way to energize employees, as everyone will attempt to do their best. The point here is not to build a comparative analysis between the two approaches but to explain that any approach will fail to produce the same results across all cultures.

Problematic Facilitators: Words and Phrases

To communicate with one another, in addition to non-verbal behaviors and expressions, we heavily rely on words and phrases. Yet, as I discussed to some extent, there are some words that can become problematic because they carry more than one meaning, some of which I will review here.

Multiple Meanings of Words

"Premium" can signify a high-quality product. In non-price promotional activities, "premium" is a product offered in addition to the product intended for sale. For example, suppose you purchased a pair of shoes. With your purchase, you received a container of shoe polish. The purpose of this, expectedly, is to entice customers to buy. However, in the insurance field, this term means a monthly (or periodic) payment.

There are many familiar words that have found their way into the world of technology. These words include "hardware," "software," "keyboard," "home," "journal," "mouse," and Internet "cookies."

In French, "moyen" means "average," and also means "a device." For example, an automobile is a "moyen" of transportation. In French, probably as in any other language, there are some words that are written almost the same way and have the same pronunciation but have completely different meanings.

- "Vers" (with a silent "s") means "toward." It also means a part of poetry.
- "Ver" means "worm."
- "Vert" (with silent "t") means green.
- "Verre" means "drinking glass."

It is interesting to note that there are words with the same spelling and pronunciation that carry different meanings depending on the context of communication. In Farsi, for example, the word "shear," can mean "milk," "lion," or "faucet."

Different Meanings of a Phrase

A manager of an international subsidiary of a U.S. firm was asked to provide data showing the sex breakdown of individuals in that organization, meaning the number of males and females. The manager responded, "… none broken down by sex….If you must know, our problem here is with alcohol." [1]

Mr. and Mrs. Smith, a host family in Boulder, Colorado, shared this experience with a guest student. An international student, who just arrived in Boulder, was eager to try a casual and traditional American meal. Mr. and Mrs. Smith and the newcomer went to a nearby hamburger restaurant. The host wanted to order a hamburger and French fries for the guest student to try. The student politely declared that he did not eat ham, considering the tenets of his religion. Although he was assured that there was no ham in the hamburger, the guest preferred to have a chicken salad instead.

Maintaining effective communication with a person from a different culture often becomes more challenging. For example, saying, "I am sorry," in one culture may commonly mean, "I made a mistake," and in another culture, it may mean "I am sorry for what has happened." The following is an illustration of such a misunderstanding.

One car ran into another car that was stopped at a red traffic light. The police officer at the scene noticed that the driver of the front car, who was a Japanese man, was saying that he was sorry, meaning that he was sorry for what had happened and not because he was at fault. However, the officer misunderstood his comment and gave him a ticket.[2]

A phrase can also be used as an expression or be taken literally, and it may have different meanings. For example, in the field of human resources, this expression could be used by an employer or an interviewer, "To work here, you really need to sell yourself," meaning that one has to demonstrate capabilities pertinent to the position. Another one is "getting up on the wrong side of the bed," meaning to be in a bad mood.

There are different expressions with basically similar meanings. In Farsi, a person having "a pebble in his shoe" means the same as someone having "something up his sleeve." Both mean that this person is being cunning or is not being truthful.

Same Words but Opposite Meanings

There was a time when the word "hot" could be used to refer to a thing or behavior that was out of the ordinary. Now, the meaning of the word "hot" has evolved to mean quite the opposite: "cool."

The word "burning" can mean to destroy, although contemporarily, the word "burning" is also used to signify making a copy. This term is commonly used to refer to making copies of CDs or DVDs, but it can also be used in other contexts. To this effect, one of my international students was working for an architectural firm as part of his internship program toward his graduate degree. One of his immediate superiors handed him a few legal-size documents and asked him to burn copies of them. The student associated the word "burn" with the word "destroy." Therefore, he thought that his superior wanted to completely get rid of the documents by burning them. This is exactly what he did. Later, when the superior found out about the confusion, it was too late.

The Intricacy of Communication in Cross-Cultural Settings

The potential for misunderstanding is always present among communicators. Intercultural communication, expectedly, is fertile ground for such a condition because of wider variations in perception, value, attitude, the meaning assigned to words, and the context in which exchanges of messages take place. For example, in England, someone might say "I hired a car," whereas in the United States, it is common to say "I rented a car." In England, someone might say, "Let's go to the cinema," which is the same as "Let's go see a movie" in the United States. Quite often, even the volume of people's voices is different from one culture to another. People in Asian countries, most notably in China and Japan, speak at a lower volume in their conversations. One of my Chinese students pointed out that the number of people living in a household in China is probably more than in most other countries. Family members sit and stand closer to each other, so a lower volume of voice is sufficient to communicate.

The point is that misunderstandings have a higher occurrence in cross-cultural settings. The real issue is how to deal with them. Recently, I have had opportunities to speak with many international

CEOs. When I asked these individuals about their biggest challenges in international settings, nearly every one of them has directed my attention to cultural understanding or, should we say, misunderstanding. One of them pointed out that we can learn about a country's environmental conditions, level of income, economic development, legal issues pertinent to international trade, GDP, GNP, and so on, but learning about culture is a whole different phenomenon.

Below we can see a short list of areas in which misunderstandings could occur in cross-cultural settings:

- How straightforward should one be, and how soon should one enter into a negotiation?
- When one party waits for the other party to initiate a business offering, does it mean the first party is less eager and will therefore have an upper hand?
- Should we take off our shoes when entering a room (for negotiation)?
- Should we shake hands, bow, or both simultaneously?
- Would it be proper to shake hands with someone of another gender?
- Is it proper to exchange gifts?
- What gift and what color would be proper?

- What should be the monetary value of the gift? An inexpensive gift could be offensive, but an expensive one might imply bribery.

- Can we rely on a firm handshake as a binding contract, or must a written document be signed?

- Does a signed contract mean the end of negotiation, or will it continue afterward, as it happens in some countries?

- What is the meaning of "yes?" Does it mean "I agree," or simply "I heard you?"

Such a list seems to be endless, so one can imagine the intricacies of cross-cultural communication in both business and interpersonal settings.

Tackling Communication in Cross-cultural Settings

The remainder of this chapter provides guidelines to alleviate misunderstandings in intercultural environments.

Active Listening

I do not know of any culture or nationality that underestimates the critical role of active listening. In most cases, one would prefer to talk rather than listen. Therefore, continual listening to another individual can become boring, particularly when there is no common interest in the topic. However, active listening has several beneficial outcomes. It indicates intelligence, the ability to concentrate, and concern for the other party and what is being said. Such caring is commonly contagious, and the other party tends to reciprocate and listen as well. Such reciprocal listening fosters friendship and will pave the road to mutual cultural understanding.

Culture-Gap Analysis

When planning to engage with individuals from different cultural backgrounds, three aspects should be considered.

First, learn about that culture as much as you reasonably can beforehand. This can be done by reading relevant books and articles, as well as by going through specific cultural training programs. If you are becoming an expatriate, chances are that your company will facilitate such programs for you. Moreover, when possible, listen to the pertinent radio stations and watch television aired from that county. This way, one can learn about the way residents interact and communicate.

Second, examine your own ability and willingness to be within a society of different values, customs, and attitudes. In many societies, for example, nibbling in a negotiation or bargaining is not uncommon after a transaction is completed. Imagine an expatriate who is assigned to live in that social environment and who does not conform to such behaviors.

Third, utilize self-experiential learning outcomes by living in a host country as a device for future international missions. An expatriate can amass considerable amounts of experience after the completion of a first mission. This practical, or hands-on experience, can be quite beneficial for the upcoming assigned missions. It is similar to learning foreign languages; once an individual learns one language, then learning another becomes easier.

Help from Translators

In an international negotiation process or for writing up a formal business contract, it is important to have a qualified translator. A translator can help ensure that each of the involved parties has a clear understanding of each specification of the negotiation. Translation is a thorny task because of the possibility of mistranslating a word or a sentence. It is therefore advisable to rely on something known as "back translation." Via this process, a contract written, for example, in Chinese, will be translated into English. Then, what has been translated into English will be translated back to Chinese. If the translation and back translation are similar, then the translation is effective.

The way people react or perceive a sentence can also make the task of translation more complicated. Often, we see owners' manuals for equipment with terms such as "DO NOT." In some cultures, such instructions would be viewed as authoritarian, and as a result, the instruction would be ignored or the product returned to the store for a refund. An alternative in this case would be a translation such as "Would you please." The dilemma is whether a translation be the exact interpretation of the original written instruction or should the translation be changed somewhat to better fit a given cultural perception.

The Wall Street Journal noted that faulty translations can have many adverse consequences, including the loss of human lives. An operator manual for a cement mixer was translated with an error that caused a pile of cement to fall on a worker in the Middle **East.**[3]

A Major Hurdle in Cross-Cultural Settings

In chapter five, we discussed ethnocentrism in relation to product standardization and adaptation. Here, we will review ethnocentrism as it relates to interacting with individuals from different cultural backgrounds, including customs, social protocols, and business conduct.

There are three outcomes of interacting with those of diverse cultures.

First, suppose Michael lives in a different culture and begins to appreciate their way of life, and begins to acquire that culture, which is known as the process of acculturation.

Second, Michael is exposed to a different culture. Regardless of whether he enjoys that culture, he successfully interacts with those of that culture without adapting to it.

Third, Michael views his culture as superior to others' cultures and establishes his culture as a standard for others to follow.

Dr. James Lee of Harvard University coined the term Self-Reference-Criterion (SRC), which refers to those who believe their culture and their way of life are superior to others. Further to this notion, those individuals fail to communicate and interact openly and successfully with those of different cultural backgrounds, which becomes a source of misunderstanding.[4]

Final Notes

Understandingly, through working and interacting with people of diverse cultural backgrounds, one will be faced with potential misunderstandings and ambiguity, but this can be an illuminating learning experience that cannot be acquired when working with people of one's own society with similar customs, language, and modes of behavior. Open-mindedness, adaptability, and appreciation of cultural variations are essential for a successful experience in the multicultural arena.

ENDNOTES

1. https://hbr.org/1973/05/how-to-choose-a-leadership-pattern

2. Jennifer J. Labbs, "Hotels Train to Help Japanese Guests," *Personnel Journal*, September 1994, p.29.

3. G. Christian Hill, "Language for Profit: More Firms Turn to Translation Experts to Avoid Costly, Embarrassing Mistakes," *The Wall Street Journal*, January 13, 1977, p. 34.

4. James Lee, *Self-Reference Criterion,* in Philip R. Cateora and John L. Graham. *International Marketing*. New York: McGraw Hill/ Irwin, 2007.

RECOMMENDED READING

John W. Santrock. Human Adjustment. New York: McGraw Hill Company, 2006.

Gary Dessler. *Human Resource Management.* Upper Saddle River, NJ: Pearson Prentice Hall, 2005.

Carl Rodrigues. *International Management: A Cultural Approach.* Cincinnati: South Western College Publishing Thomas Learning, 2001.

Richard W. Brislin, *Cross-Cultural Encounters.* New York: Pergamon Press, 1982.

Ronald B. Adler and Neil Towne. *Looking Out/ Looking In: Interpersonal Communication.* Fort Worth, TX: Harcourt Brace College Publisher, 1993.

Glossary

Comfort Zone is a psychological condition where a person experiences no or minimal level of stress and frustration.

Emerging Markets are countries that are positioning themselves to transition from developing to developed economies.

Ethnocentrism is the belief that one's own culture, customs, and way of life are superior to those of others.

Franchising occurs when a company licenses its intellectual property rights, such as its name, logo, and production methods, to another company in exchange for compensation, such as 10 percent of total revenue, known as royalties.

Gross Domestic Product (GDP) is the total value of all goods and services produced *within* a given country. For example, the Toyota Camry production plant in Georgetown, Kentucky, contributes to the GDP of the United States.

Gross National Product (GNP) refers to the total value of all goods and services produced *by* a country, regardless of where the production takes place. For example, an iPhone, which is manufactured by the American company Apple in China, is included in the GNP of the United States.

Groupthink is a phenomenon that compromises effective group decision-making by pressuring members to achieve consensus.

Job Orientation refers to the process of helping new hires feel comfortable by familiarizing them with their tasks, duties, and the working environment.

Information Overload happens when a person receives too many tasks and instructions, making it difficult to process them effectively.

Per Capita Income refers to the average income earned by each individual in a specific country or market. It is calculated by dividing the total income earned by the population of that country or market.

Perception is how an individual views reality.

Random Sampling Random sampling is when each individual or object in a population has the same probability of being selected.

Index

D

E

F

G

Just in Time, 6

K, L

Kennedy International Airport, 55
Kitcatt, 130
KLM, 56-7, 182
Kodak, 6
Kotler, Philip, 121-2
Laissez-faire leadership, 104, 188
Levitt, Theodore, 121
Liechtenstein, 9
Listening, 62, 97, 117, 159, 197-8
Literacy, level of, 140-1
LL Bean, 99
Low Context Culture (LCC), 4, 31
Lubrication, 173

M

Macroenvironment, 104, 106-8
Malaysia, 42
Management effectiveness, 103
Manners, 24-5, 38
Marasmus, 18
Marketing decisions, 141, 182
Marketing research, 117-8, 173
Maslow, A. H., 95
Messages, 13, 36, 38-9, 45, 56, 59, 60
Mexico, 8, 131, 157
Microenvironment, 104-5, 108, 110
Middle East, the, 20, 42, 160
Misleading information, 89

Misleading pricing, 126
Misleading volume, 123
Mission statement, 81, 83-4

N

National perspective, 8
New York, 55
Newstrom, John W., 63
Nibbling, 169
Nodding, 38-9
Noise, 15
Nordstrom, 99, 120
North America, 39
North American, 8, 137
North American Free Trade Agreement (NAFTA), 8
Northwestern University, 121
Norway, 9
Nudity, 138

O P

Organization(s), 6-8
Pakistan, 4, 40, 163
Pan American, 57
Per capita income, 5, 140-1, 178
Peru, 54
Political, 107, 170-1
Projection, 85-6
Promotion, 89, 129, 134
Protocol(s), 3, 23, 66, 68-9, 145, 159, 161-2, 167,
   178, 200

Q R

S

www.ingramcontent.com/pod-product-compliance
Lightning Source LLC
Chambersburg PA
CBHW071117280326
41935CB00010B/1043